50p

GW01066218

22 JUL 1985

WITHDRAWN
FROM THE
CITY OF WESTMINSTER
PUBLIC LIBRARIES

SOLD

Malcolm John   Drawings by C.A.T. Brigden

Around Historic Kent

MIDAS BOOKS

WESTMINSTER
CITY LIBRARIES

The Illustrator

C.A.T. BRIGDEN was born in Rochester in 1908.

He was educated at Sir Joseph Williamson's Mathematical School, Rochester, and at Goldsmith's College, New Cross, London, where he specialised in Art and History.

He became Head of the Art Department at Highfield School, Chatham, after serving with the RAF 1942-1945. Since his retirement from teaching he has been engaged in painting and illustrating, having had many successful one-man shows in Kent.

His hobbies are painting and golf.

In the same illustrated series
Around Historic Sussex by Ray Miller and Gerald Lip
Around Historic Hampshire by Colin Wintle and Victor Spink
Around Historic Yorkshire by Jeffrey Lee and Les Coldrick
Around Historic Lancashire by David Jessop
Around Historic Somerset and Avon by Colin Wintle and Nicola
    Luscombe
Around the Historic Chilterns by Ron Pigram
Around Historic Devon and Cornwall by Desmond Post and Stuart
    Richmond

First published 1978 by
MIDAS BOOKS
12 Dene Way, Speldhurst,
Tunbridge Wells, Kent, TN3 0NX

© Malcolm John and C.A.T. Brigden 1978
All rights reserved. No part of this publication may be reproduced, stored in a retrieval system, or transmitted in any form or by any means electronic, mechanical, photocopying, recording or otherwise, without the prior permission of Midas Books.

ISBN 0 85936 107 1
17901   942.23T

Typeset by 900 Characters, Edenbridge, Kent.
Printed in Great Britain by Tonbridge Printers, Tonbridge, Kent.

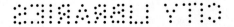

CONTENTS
AND
ILLUSTRATIONS

ALLINGTON CASTLE

Allington Castle, lying as it does on the non-tidal bend of the
Medway, enjoys an idyllic setting. The overgrown greystone ruins,
the presence of doves and the quiet industry of the priests lend a
restful atmosphere. The castle, run now by the Carmelites who
occupy The Friars at Aylesford some two miles downstream, has a
long and fascinating history.

Defence was always a prime consideration and Sir William de
Warenne made the castle so impregnable that Henry II later
demanded its demolition! Later in 1282-3, after an unfortified manor
had been constructed on the site, Edward I permitted Stephen de
Penchester to rebuild the castle defensively and it was he who added
the Penchester Wings, including the Great Hall.

The castle was bought by the Wyatt family in 1492 and
restoration was begun. Important visitors to Allington included the
Tudor monarchs, their queens and officers and, perhaps most
interestingly, Anne Boleyn. Sir Thomas Wyatt, the great Elizabethan
poet, lived out his life at Allington.

Sir Thomas Wyatt's son, also a Sir Thomas, was executed in
1554 for taking part in the rising against Mary Tudor. The castle
then reverted to the Crown, and having passed through many hands,
fell into semi-ruin, to be restored in the twentieth century by Lord
Conway. It is now a retreat and daughter house of the Carmelite
Friary at Aylesford.

APPLEDORE

The south-east coast of Kent has from time immemorial borne the
brunt of foreign invasion. Romans, Scandinavians and Normans with
considerable success plundered the area; within the last 250 years
French and Germans have constituted similar dangers.

The coast today still bears reminders of the Napoleonic threats
upon our island. The sprinkling of Martello towers and the splendid
Royal Military Canal stretching as it does from Hythe almost to
Hastings thirty miles distant, impress upon the observer the serious
nature of those threats. The latter made possible the defensive
deployment of troops along its waterways. Constructed at a cost of
£250,000 it was not completed until after the Battle of Trafalgar
when it may be argued the invasion threat had passed.

During the nineteenth century charges were levied upon barge
traffic using the canal but increasing road and rail competition in the
1840s and 1850s led to reductions in trade and revenue and today it
is simply used by pleasure craft.

Inland from the coastal town of Hythe en route to Rye are the
villages of Bilsington, Ruckinge and Appledore. The latter has a
charming thirteenth century church and a pleasant rural air although
its smock windmill has now gone. At Hornes Place there is a fine
timber-framed house with licensed chapel dated 1366 constructed
principally of ragstone.

ASHFORD

Ashford has recently fallen victim to the planners. Designated a
growth area it has spawned the inevitable modern housing estates
and a ring road which has suffocated the formerly quite pleasant
centre of this small market town.

Ashford came of age during the railway boon years of the last
century when it became not only an important rail junction but a
principal centre of engine and rolling stock manufacture. Now, in
spite of central shopping developments, it remains essentially the
focus of local agricultural trade with a flourishing weekly market.

Architecturally, the town's chief interest lies within the few square
yards enclosing the church, namely the former college buildings with
their narrow alleyways not unlike the 'Lanes' at Brighton. Whilst the
town may not, therefore, be remarkable for its outstanding historical
dwellings, many of the buildings in the older shopping areas reveal a
substantial past.

7

AYLESFORD 1

Aylesford, with its oft-sketched and photographed bridge, is unfortunately not the picturesque village of former times. Road traffic and river pollution are ever present village problems. The former constitutes a considerable threat to some fine timber-framed buildings such as the former George Inn, now a private residence, a Grade I listed fourteenth century construction.

Aylesford Bridge has a wide central arch with pedestrian refuges or buttresses. The whole structure groans with a constant stream of vehicles although some relief is afforded by a modern counterpart of temporary construction.

The Bridge

AYLESFORD 2

Aylesford, known as the 'Cradle of English History', has a long,
interesting association with The Friars. The Carmelite Order was
originally brought here from Mount Carmel in Palestine by Baron
Richard de Gray of Codnor — legend has it that their occupation
began on Christmas Day in 1240. The Baron gave his Aylesford
manor to these monks on his return from the Crusades. They were
given every encouragement by the Bishop of Rochester and the
church was dedicated in 1245 with the splendid title, 'Assumption of
the Glorious Virgin'. The first pilgrimage or world visitation to
Aylesford was in 1247 when the first chapter was held and St Simon
Stock elected Prior General.

The order then adopted the title 'Mendicant Friars', their
importance grew and centres were established in Oxford, Cambridge
and London. By the time of the dissolution of the monastries in
1538, there were over forty such centres. The subsequent history of
The Friars was somewhat chequered, passing from Sir Thomas
Wyatt in the sixteenth century through various owners until it
eventually came into the possession of the Earl of Aylesford.

The Carmelite Order purchased the building after it had been
partially damaged by fire in 1930.

The Priory

BARFRESTON

The Church at Barfreston has received high acclaim for its superb south doorway which dates from the twelfth century. The total building comprises a nave and chancel and is quite small. It is constructed of flint and Caen stone ashlar. There is much carving, mostly original, with the exception of Hussey's restoration after subsidence had occurred (see *Archaeologia Cantiana* Vol XVI).

The church has no tower, and the bell hangs nearby in a yew tree. The many sculptures cover mouldings, doorways and walls, and include fantasies in stone, birds, animals, and people. It is possible that many have allegorical meanings that date from a past older than the church, and which we no longer comprehend.

BAYHAM ABBEY

The remains of this Premonstratensian Abbey are near Lamberhurst, and are the property of the Marquis Camden. At the Dissolution of the Monasteries, Bayham was assigned to Cardinal Wolsey, there then being but five canons, in addition to the abbot. On the fall of Wolsey, the abbey reverted to the Crown, but in Queen Elizabeth's reign, the property was granted in part to Viscount Montague, and the remainder to Robert Adams, grocer. It later passed to John Pratt, Esq,. Sergeant-at-law, later Chief Justice of the King's Bench. His third son was the 1st Earl Camden, and Lord High Chancellor of England.

Bayham Abbey

BEARSTED

Bearsted, now a suburb of Maidstone and with the inevitable rash of building developments, has nevertheless some redeeming features and is close by Bearsted Green.

The Green has several interesting, timbered dwellings which overlook the village green where cricket may occasionally be enjoyed.

Here played the great nineteenth century cricketer Alfred Mynn, the Lion of Kent. The golf course was opened in 1923 by the celebrated golfer, Harry Vardon. The fourteenth century church is noted for its fine tower and timbered roof. The former has 3 curious beasts looking out over the parish. Here is buried Sir Thomas Fludd, scholar, philosopher and occult scholar, and son of Sir Thomas Fludd, Treasurer to Elizabeth I. In Bearsted lives Baroness Orczy, who wrote the famous Scarlet Pimpernel stories.

The River Len wanders through the parish but, unfortunately, does not touch upon the village.

The River Len

BEXLEYHEATH

The Red House at Bexleyheath was the country house of William Morris. Research informs us that the house was designed by Philip Webb following a trip to observe the medieval cathedrals along the banks of the River Seine in 1858. It is said that Rossetti was unable to find words to describe adequately the completed building — Morris's medieval folly. However, it proved to be a milestone in English domestic architecture.

The house is red-bricked with red tiles and acutely pitched roofs. There are gables and tall chimneystacks. Parts of the fabric and the windows are designed more appropriately for a chapel or school hall than for a home. There are numerous interesting features including a minstrels' gallery, a splendid ceiling, home-made furniture and misplaced stained-glass windows.

Bexleyheath is now within the boundaries of Greater London.

The Red House

Old Cloth Hall

BIDDENDEN

The much visited Wealden village of Biddenden has a delightful high street. A splendid cloth hall and weavers' building dominate this area and the attics of the shops on the south side run the length of the building. It is not surprising that we should encounter evidence of an earlier textile trade here since Biddenden was the weaving centre of the Kentish woollen industry based at Cranbrook and Tenterden in the seventeenth century.

The wide and irregular pavements are made from Bethersden marble whilst there is a fine thirteenth century church with some splendid brasses.

The village sign showing two ladies depicts the Siamese twins Eliza and Mary Chulkhurst, of the 12th century who lived in the village to about the age of 34 years when one of them died. The other died shortly after her sister. They bequeathed lands known as the Bread and Cheese Lands to charity, for the use of the poor. The charity still exists, but much doubt has been cast upon the story of the two sisters insofar as they were Siamese twins.

BOUGHTON MONCHELSEA

We are at Boughton Monchelsea truly in the Garden of England, traditionally agricultural Kent, where the village church of St Peter's is remarkable for its lychgate, rose trees and extensive views across the Weald.

The old ragstone quarries not many yards distant offer a sharp contrast with their rugged appearance. They indeed provided the material for Westminster Abbey and, later, war reparations to the Houses of Parliament. In the early days of artillery, the stone was dressed to form cannon balls.

Within the parish is Boughton Monchelsea Place, a mansion set in parkland dating from the mid-sixteenth century but extensively altered and rebuilt some three hundred years later. Close by the quarries one may find the site of a Roman villa bath house.

BOXLEY

Boxley although no longer quite so rural as formerly still has a charm of its own. In the church are memorials to the Lushington family, and here is buried Tennyson's sister Cecilia wife of Edmund Lushington. A small brook that feeds a lake near Sandling is reputedly the one in Tennyson's poem. The remains of Boxley Abbey walls cover a wide area, and the house on the site of the old Abbey is probably 18th century. In an earlier day the Abbey was noted for two wonderworking images, the Rood of Boxley, and a figure of St Romwold both of which brought in many contributions to the monks from the credulous. The great barn may have been the guesting house in monastic days. The ancient Chapel of St Andrews, now a private house is twelfth century.

In Boxley is Park House, seat of the Best family, once occupied by Tennyson. At the southern end of the village lie the remains of Boxley Abbey founded in the twelfth century by the Earl of Kent, William de Ypres.

The building, the only Cistercian Abbey in Kent, has witnessed some recent excavation.

The Church

BRENCHLEY

The Weald of Kent, arguably the heart of the county, has bred many important people including the first English printer, William Caxton, and from Brenchley, William Lambarde who wrote the Perambulation of Kent. This was the first county history to have been written and has stood the test of time, being reprinted in about eight editions, all revising the original work completed in 1576. Lambarde lived for a time at Brattles Grange, a half-timbered building built about 1500 which subsequently passed into the hands of Nelson's family.

The village of Brenchley, set on a hillside, has many timbered buildings in the Tudor black and white style, including the butcher's shop and the Old Palace, restored and built in traditional Wealden manner.

Many of the buildings bear interesting names, Brenchley Manor and Marle Place, half-timbered sixteenth and seventeenth century dwellings being good examples. In general the reader would be rewarded by looking at the recently completed county planning department's village study.

BROADSTAIRS

A short walk along Fort Road will reward the visitor with a sight of Bleak House. Constructed in 1801 under the original name of Fort House, one of its early owners was one George Gouch, captain of the Loyal Cinque Ports Volunteers and commander of the North Cliff Battery established at the start of the Napoleonic Wars.

The site of the old Tudor fort next to the house was enlarged and a telegraph station constructed. In 1901 the name of the house was changed to Bleak House and even Dickens, a frequent visitor to Broadstairs in former times, would not have recognised it.

The author wrote *Pickwick Papers, Oliver Twist, Nicholas Nickleby* and *David Copperfield* whilst at Broadstairs. He especially liked the tiny beach and harbour and yearned to buy Bleak House from Wilkie Collins. The house rewards the tourist visitor with the author's study, chair and other memorabilia.

BROOKLAND

Brookland is a gem in the tranquil marshlands of south-eastern Kent.
The central point of the hamlet is the church with its detached belfry.
This is not a downland ragstone church but a structure primarily of
wood. The belfry is entirely wooden and octagonal in shape. It
comprises three stages about thirty-five feet by sixty feet high, and
this staging is believed to be restricted mainly to Kentish churches.
The church itself is a mixture of architectural styles dating from the
thirteenth century. The most important feature inside the church is
the font which is of Norman origin and in lead, with the zodiacal
signs and labours of the month in two rows in Latin and French.
The church has survived both Victorian church restoration and war
damage. An old story accounts for the detached belfry by the fact
that in former days few people bothered to marry, and when a couple
did come to the church for this purpose, the belfry was so startled
that it leapt down to its present position.

19

BURHAM

Burham Village nestles at the foot of the North Downs and stands on the Pilgrims' Way between Chatham and Maidstone. The River Medway wanders nearby and there was once a ferry from Snodland, doubtless taking pilgrims en route to Canterbury via this shorter way.

The Old Church stands somewhat forlorn by the edge of the river, but has been restored. In the churchyard was once a tombstone with a twisted face on it, and the words beneath,

> Behold Burham's Belle, a delight,
> With her curls assymetric and tight;
> Let us hope that her Biz,
> Was as straight as her Phiz,
> And she kept like her Nose to the
> Right.

A new church was built some half mile distant as part of the expanding village pattern.

The Old Church

CANTERBURY 1

Canterbury is the ecclesiastical capital of England. Ever since the
early landings and Ethelbert, the King of Kent's confirmation of land
for the Cathedral Area in 597, not to mention the Becket legend, the
city has become a shrine visited by thousands of British and
foreigners each year.

Ethelbert's gift enabled St Augustine to establish the cathedral
within the town walls and the abbey outside. The abbey was
originally dedicated to St Peter and St Paul to be later generally
abandoned in favour of St Augustine himself. The occupants had
considerable independence and importance, the abbot having a seat
in the House of Lords and the monks showing allegiance to no one
but the Pope.

With the exception of the gateways and guest house, the abbey
has suffered rather more, structurally, than the cathedral. Recently,
the whole ground floor has been excavated revealing its construction
plan. The building has a curious history of occupation since,
following the dissolution of the monastries, it has had royal
inhabitants, followed by Lord Woolton and the famous Hales family.
Now in use at St Augustine's College, it was also once a brewery.

CANTERBURY 2

The Dane John is a curious relic of antiquity even for Canterbury. In the centre of the feature is a large mound which was possibly a Danish burial mound. The present height, however, dates only from the late eighteenth century when a local benefactor transformed the area into a 'pleasure garden' and planted the now infamous avenue of lime trees.

Within the walls were to be seen a capstan reputed to have been removed from Nelson's flagship, "Foudroyant", and at one end by the roundabout can be seen George Stephenson's locomotive, "Invicta", constructed in 1825 and used on the difficult route of the Canterbury and Whitstable railway from 1830.

Other memorials include those of the Buffs who perished fighting in the South African War (the local East Kent Regiment) and Canterbury's famous playwright, Christopher Marlowe, whose name is given to the city's theatre. Directly opposite the gardens stands the Norman castle keep, now one storey shorter than the original and from which an excellent view of the city can be obtained.

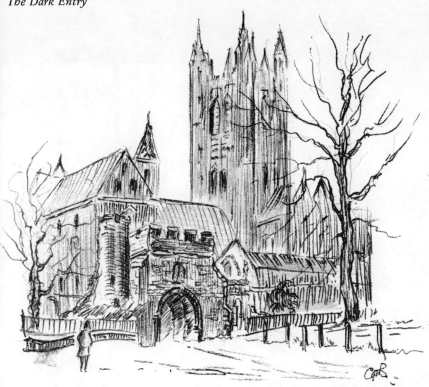

CANTERBURY 3

Under the direction of Archbishop Lanfranc, Canterbury was made the largest monastery in England with a total of 150 monks. Their buildings were constructed on the northern side of the cathedral and included the usual quarters of cloister, chapter house and dormitory/refectory. They were extensive and externally forbidding, being windowless up to the Gate.

This area, designated "Dark Entry" to the cathedral, was made famous by the Ingoldsby Legends, being the place where Nell Cook's ghost appears.

Inside is the tranquil Green Court, the Deanery on the right and, at the end, 'Chittenden House' dating from the time of the Normans. This is the King's School country and some of the hustle and bustle of the commercial world is transformed to meet the needs of the growing youth — a fitting contrast to the staid and solid foundation of the cathedral, its Norman architecture and centuries of tradition.

CANTERBURY 4

Mercery Lane gives the pilgrim a glimpse of the cosiness of medieval street life where neighbours across the street could shake hands from the upstairs windows of the overhanging upper storeys.

There are two alleys now remaining in Kent known to the author which suggest this Tudor fashion, both in cathedral cities, namely, Mercery Lane and Two Post Alley at Rochester.

The whole of the western side of Mercery Lane was one building, the Chequers Inn, now comprising nine buildings which afforded accommodation for 100 pilgrims and a few merrymakers!

The superb view of the cathedral before one passes beneath the Christchurch Gate prepares one for the greater glories of the interior of the cathedral, the Martyrdom, the Black Prince's tomb, and the Warriors Chapel, to name but a few of the monuments and treasures to be seen.

CANTERBURY 5

Canterbury can be divided into many tours and the city wall exhaust all but the most adventurous investigator. The obvious centre of attraction is the cathedral from where the routes spread in all directions to the North Gate, via Palace Street, the King's School and John Boys House, the castle and the Dane John, the Weavers and the West Gate.

How many pilgrims, however, find the time or energy to pass through the massive arch of the West Gate? Hundreds of students walk the streets of St Dunstan's Without en route to the university high on the hill along the Whitstable road. The initial exploration will be fruitful, for the stretch of buildings from the West Gate to the railway line is worthy of inspection. One of the best known is the House of Agnes, the Agnes Wickfield of *David Copperfield* who met David, when his aunt Miss Betsy Trotwood brought him here to live with Agnes and her father, when David attended the King's School. Almost opposite is the Falstaff Inn, and St Dunstan's Church is also worthy of inspection, time permitting.

St Dunstan's Street

CANTERBURY 6

The twin towers of the West Gate stand strong and firm, albeit congested with traffic, and passed by countless students wearily climbing Whitstable Hill on their way back to the university overlooking the city.

The present structure dates only from 1380. Situated on the Stour the West Gate defended the city against water borne attack, and had its drawbridge and portcullis, arrowslit windows and other defences. At one period it was used as a prison, and the condemned cell may still be seen in the museum housed in the towers.

This gateway is a good clean example of ragstone construction, affording protection through the centuries to St Peter's Street and the commercial areas of Canterbury.

CHARING

Nestling at the foot of the North Downs, Charing has unfortunately become a mere road junction where the roads divide from Maidstone to Ashford or Canterbury. Travellers on both roads could easily miss the short high street, which has several old buildings worthy of study, along with the church and the ruins of the Tudor Archbishop's Palace.

The tower of the church is typically Kentish, built of ragstone and attached to the church which is principally Early English. Rumour has it that the roof was burned down in the reign of Henry VIII by a man shooting at a pigeon, but was hurriedly rebuilt for a visit made by Queen Elizabeth to the Archbishop's Palace en route to the cathedral at Canterbury. Before entering the church door, note the tombstone to the memory of Quarter Master Thomas Loftus. He was wounded at Bunker's Hill, and served in the 52nd Foot for many years.

On returning to the main road, time should be taken to inspect the overhanging, timber-framed buildings together with several other houses of a later date.

27

CHARTHAM

There is little to recommend Chartham to the visitor or explorer. The village lies on the Pilgrims' route to Canterbury and can only be described as disappointing in contrast to the charming village of Chilham.

The valley of the River Stour is worth following and, although there are mills and a chancel at Chartham, the raped Forest of Blean which originally stretched to the Whitstable coast is more interesting to study.

The church is very large and was built mainly in the fourteenth century. Internally, it has been restored and the 'Kentish' traceried windows have been cleaned. There are several small brasses worth inspecting and, nearby, some half-timbered houses and a medieval chapel at Horton.

The Mill Chartham

CHARTWELL

Chartwell is a pleasant house situated a mile or so south of Westerham where General Wolfe's 'Quebec House' and statue may be seen.

Chartwell was, of course, the country retreat of Sir Winston Churchill, and the house remains a treasure trove of Churchilliana. The house is now maintained by the National Trust and holds many of Sir Winston's paintings and military photographs. The great statesman very frequently turned to painting in the Chartwell grounds as a welcome relief from the daily stress of political life.

A stone statue erected in 1969 in nearby Westerham remembers Sir Winston as a local resident.

Chartwell

CHATHAM 1

The sea and navy, the dockyard and Fort Pitt, are of course the roots of Chatham. Nevertheless, the town does have very close, though less well-known, links with Charles Dickens. At an early age the author's family brought him to live in the terrace of houses near the station. Known as No. 2 Ordnance Terrace, there was nothing remarkable about the house which is now a mere shell.

The intention to create a Dickens' museum came to nought and, with the author's other Chatham house in the Brook close to St Mary's Church falling into disrepair, the memory of the great writer seems rapidly to be fading.

30   *Ordnance Terrace*

CHATHAM 2

Chatham was a natural docking place lying in the sheltered waters of the River Medway below Rochester, the ancient city and crossing place of the river. The Hoo Peninsula curves eastwards towards the North Sea establishing a sheltered channel, and it was here that the medieval monarchs based their navy and established a shipbuilding yard. Materials, mainly wood, were easily accessible from the Weald of Kent's forest, as were iron and cheap labour. Today's dockyard is very different. Gone are the wooden ships, the great ironclads and even submarines. A small elite of nuclear experts work here but the yard always fears closure orders from the Ministry of Defence. It was along this stretch by Riverside that the Dutch Admiral — de Ruyter — attacked Medway in 1667, setting fire to many of the warships lying at anchor. It was then that a chain was placed on the sea bed against future attacks and additional defence works were undertaken at Upnor Castle.

The splendid St Mary's church, magnificently sited, faces a similar fight against demolition with the Church Commissioners, and could be a maritime centre of Medway.

The Riverside Chatham

CHEVENING

Chevening Place, amid its beautiful acres of woodland, was formerly the home of the Stanhope family. Built in the early 17th century, in the style of Inigo Jones, this impressive house is now occupied by H. M. Prince Charles, The Prince of Wales.

The house, constructed of warm red brick, is typical of its period, although it was remodelled in the early 18th century. Additions to the original building include the Library Wing which was intended to accommodate fifteen thousand books.

The Stanhope Chapel houses the tombs of many former owners including the Elizabethan Lennards. The men of this family were buried with their armour and the women in the costumes of the period. One of the more notable of the Stanhopes to be buried here is Charles Stanhope, a politician who married William Pitt's sister.

Chevening was unoccupied for some time after the death of the last of the Stanhopes who bequeathed the house to the nation. In view of its present occupier, the estate is hardly likely to be engulfed in a modern housing development, unlike the nearby Chipstead Place.

Chevening

CHIDDINGSTONE

Chiddingstone Castle is a sham, with its huge gateway looking like
Battle Abbey and battlements dating from the start of the nineteenth
century rising over a seventeenth century manor house. There were
originally two manors, one the property of the well-known de
Cobhams, which passed to the Burghs and then to the Streatfield
family.

The county of Sussex was represented by the other manor, and the
family Burghest were in residence from the thirteenth century and
provided one constable of Dover Castle and Lord Warden of the
Cinque Ports; also a grandson who fought for Edward II. In
1700 the Streatfields purchased the manor, thus owning at that time
most of Chiddingstone. Set in a beautiful background, much of the
property belongs to the National Trust, attracting many visitors, and
is mainly Tudor, or Elizabethan. In the park is a great sarsen called
the Chiding Stone, and it is thought that this may have been the
centre of some bygone worship in ancient days.

CHILHAM

Chilham has the perfect village square, quaint houses and, predominantly, the church. Close by there is a Norman castle where medieval banquets and feasts are held regularly. From each entrance the square is enchanting, marred only by the inevitable cars.

The church, dedicated to St Mary, has a perpendicular flint west tower with octagonal turret and heavily constructed weathervane. Inside the church there are several monuments made of the Bethersden marble which lines the peculiar streets of old Biddenden.

The heronry in the park is said to date from the thirteenth century, and not far away is a long barrow of Neolithic origin with a Roman burial at one end, which may or may not be the grave of Julius Laberius. The mound is locally called Juliberrie's Grave.

The Norman castle was built and rebuilt several times over the centuries. The castle played an important defensive role and was of unusual design — an octagonal keep with a solid curtain wall. Internally, the hall and staircases are the most attractive features.

This place, Chilham, was a favourite resting place on all pilgrimages to Canterbury.

34

COBHAM 1

Cobham is a village with a park, a large house, several minor
buildings, a church which excels in its brasses, and some good
hostelries. *A Yeoman of Kent* by Ralph Arnold charts the history
of the Hayes, a Cobham family.

The one long village street from Cobham Park to Owletts is
worthy of close inspection and was surveyed in the planning
booklet which includes all the listed buildings. The most
photographed building is the Leather Bottle, wellknown to all
lovers of Dickens's *Pickwick Papers*. Dickens took much
pleasure in the area, and made a point of taking foreign friends to
the village.

The almshouses of Cobham College, however, are original. The
college was founded by Sir John de Cobham in 1362 and the
buildings were down-graded to almshouses about 1600. These
buildings were centred around the church of St Mary which is very
large and beautiful and has possibly the best brasses in a village
church in the whole county. A booklet is available in the church
which is also well described in Pevsner's guide to West Kent and
the Weald. Owletts, the manor house just along from the church
was built in 1683 but has modern additions by a later owner, Sir
Herbert Baker.

The Leather Bottle

COBHAM 2

Cobham Hall, set in its own parkland, is as attractive to the eye today as it would have appeared upon its completion about the year 1602. From a modest design of a manor house, it was transformed into a magnificent Tudor mansion. The transformation was undertaken by William Brooke. Further additions were made between 1662 and 1670 including a central section and the western face, built by John Webb. Alterations to the building continued and, whilst James Repton was undertaking the landscaping of the gardens and formal layout of the park. It is said that he was responsible for the maintenance of the avenue of lime trees, one thousand yards long, spreading towards the village.

The Darnleys are possibly the best known owners of Cobham Hall, which is now a girls' public school. Although the family mausoleum in the park has never been used it is unfortunately much vandalised.

Cobham Hall

COOLING

Cooling is 'Pip's Village' for here in the remote churchyard are the strange lozenge-shaped tombstones or gravestones known to Pip in *Great Expectations,* by Charles Dickens. The church, situated on a knot in the road, is in fourteenth century ragstone with a plain but pleasant interior. Unfortunately, the building is now unused due to dwindling congregations.

Just a short distance along the lane is Cooling Castle with its impressive twin-towered gatehouse. John de Cobham was granted a licence to fortify his manor house at Cooling in 1381 following French raids on the area a few years previously. It seems unfortunate that there has to be a modern house adjacent to the ruined walls of the castle. There is a fine farm stone building to the right of the gate house which is open to the rear with turrets at the top and arrowslits for archers.

To reassure the people that his castle was not built to over-awe them, Sir John de Cobham added a plaque with a seal attached, to one of the towers, which read:

Knouweth that beth and schul be
That I am mad in help of the cuntre
In knowyng at whyche thyng
Thy is charte and wytnessyng.

37

CRANBROOK

Cranbrook is a capital of the Kentish Weald and the church has
been called the 'Cathedral of the Weald.'

    Cranbrook has many fine varied period buildings and from most
parts of the village one may see the white-painted sails of the
Union Mill. The mill is situated just off one of the main shopping
streets — Stone Street by St David's Bridge — and is reputed to be
the largest smock mill in the south of England. When the owner
retired in the mid-fifties, its future was uncertain but £2500 was
raised for its preservation and maintenance. Its restoration was
entrusted to some famous Dutch millwrights but it seldom operates
now. The sweep of the mill has an approximately seventy feet span.
The mill was originally built for Henry Dobell in 1814.

    The charm of Cranbrook's townscape is the tile-hung
weatherboarded cottages, both in shops and houses where
traditional crafts and occupations are encouraged.

DARTFORD

Dartford takes its name from the ancient ford that crossed the river Darent. Historically, the settlement's significance stems from the river crossing the mud flats and marshes, joining with the river Cray on its way to the Thames.

The Holy Trinity Church dates from Norman times, the period that is mirrored in the north tower and the buttresses. Later additions include a perpendicular chapel and a late 14th century west aisle. Now only the tower remains from the Norman original.

The nearby priory was occupied by Dominican nuns, who were established there by Edward III in 1346.

Wat Tyler's insurrection began at Dartford in 1381.

After the Dissolution of the Monasteries, the Courtyard House was built (1541-44) to give facilities to Henry VIII when travelling along the London-Dover road.

England's first rolling and slitting mill for iron was built here in the 16th century and, in Victorian times, Dartford possessed powder mills, locomotive machinery and chemical works, corn mills and breweries.

The few ancient buildings that remain in Dartford are mainly in Bullace Lane. But for the visitors' appreciation there is the Royal Victoria Bull Hotel which, like its namesake in Rochester, was a coaching inn; no doubt visited by Charles Dickens on his perambulations.

Holy Trinity, Dartford

DODE

Dode Church is disused as the former congregations now travel to St Peter and St Paul at Luddesdown, a mile and a half distant. The church at Dode was small with a Norman nave and now overgrown churchyard. There is debate over the originality of the flints and dressing stones because Pevsner says it was restored in 1905-6, and yet Finch quotes the booklet about Dode by Arnold as saying, "...it never at any time had been handed over to any spoiler, nor has the restorer ever set his mark upon it."

It is said that during the Black Death about 1349, the complete population was wiped out, and history records in 1367 that no person had resided in the parish for over 15 years. The original dedication of the church remains a mystery and the building has always been associated with that of Paddlesworth. The incumbents must of necessity have administered both isolated buildings.

A fuller description of the church can be found in the magnificent *Customale Roffense,* depicting the buildings and the history of the ecclesiastical jurisdiction of the Rochester Diocese.

Much of the antiquity of the area can be discovered by reading William Coles-Finch's delightful book, *In Kentish Pilgrim Land.*

DOVER

Dover Castle perfectly illustrates the value of strategic siting,
perched loftily on the cliffs overlooking the harbour. There have been
defensive sites here at least since Roman times with evidence in the
form of the 'Pharos' or Roman Lighthouse.

Dover was of great importance during the Norman Conquest and
much blood must have been spilled before the Normans built their
massive stone-walled keep.

A tour of the castle area will reveal architectural styles dating
from the reign of Henry II. By the time of his death, over £6000 had
been spent on fortifications — a massive sum in medieval terms.
From the twelfth century the keep and inner curtain walls were built,
and part of the outer curtain walls. Outward projecting towers gave
added security along with fourteen round towers and two gateways.
A new gate, built after 1216 and called Constable's Tower, can be
seen in the sketch. The gate now forms the entrance by the road to
the castle.

41

EAST FARLEIGH

The tiny village of East Farleigh, standing on the banks of the River Medway, has a magnificent medieval stone bridge comprising five arches. History records that at the time of the Civil War, Fairfax and his troops crossed this bridge on their way to capture Maidstone, some two miles to the east, from the Royalists. As though by artistic chance, there are several oasts and drying kilns for the locally grown hops. Near to this village are the Whitbread Hop Farms.

The church has a Norman tower and a nave and chancel dating from the thirteenth century. There is also a monument to William Wilberforce who did so much to abolish slavery.

There was once a splendid half-timbered building called Court Lodge in the parish but, in order to escape demolition, it had to be moved and re-erected as part of the Maidstone Museum; clearly here the countryman's loss is the townsman's gain.

Here is buried Donald Maxwell, author of many books on a variety of subjects, including Kent. There is also a monument to 43 hop-pickers who died of the cholera here in 1849.

The Bridge

EAST MALLING

All that seems to be missing from East Malling is a village green and a pond. The side approach of Church Walk with its trees on the north side and the heavily-timbered antique shop opposite complete an attractive picture. The church was rebuilt by Bishop Gundulf, of Rochester over 800 years ago, and in it lie, amongst others, Sir Thomas Twysden, one of those who judged the regicide judges of Charles I. The old home of the Twysden's is now part of the East Malling Research Station.

The church indeed has memorials to the Twisden family who were occupants of Bradbourne from its construction in 1713, this being officially within the Larkfield parish.

Returning to the main London road one should not miss the group of sixteenth century cottages straddling the traffic lights. Painted blue, the most westerly building is an old wheel-wright's cottage and still contains many interesting features, including tools and equipment of the trade.

St James' Church

EYNSFORD AND LULLINGSTONE

Several old timber-framed houses make up a tranquil picture postcard setting here on the Darent.

Here also Eynsford Castle is located, once the possession of Christchurch, Canterbury, and later of the great Norman archbishop, Lanfranc. The castle was fortified during Norman times owing to the proximity of Bishop Odo of Bayeux, the Earl of Kent. The castle was variously occupied by William de Eynsford III during the reign of Henry II and by Ralph de Farningham in 1264. Indirectly it passed circa 1520 to the Lullingstone Estate of the Harts when it became derelict until preservation was carried out during the early part of the century.

Nearby is Lullingstone Castle, built on the site of the original manor house of the Domesday Survey, and largely rebuilt in the eighteenth century. The gateway dating from Henry VIII's reign still remains. The castle contains fine Tudor panelling and a collection of armour and paintings.

The excavation of Lullingstone Villa has revealed a Roman country house and Christian chapel. A mosaic floor laid in the fourth century is one of many fine decorative features.

The Ford, Eynsford

FAVERSHAM

At the time of the dissolution of the monastries, Faversham Abbey passed into the hands of the Lord Warden of the Cinque Ports, one Sir Thomas Cheney. There were at that time considerable revenues attached to these estates in Kent.

In the bureaucracy of the Tudor king's parliament, there was a clerk named Thomas Arderne (Arden) who by devious means was created Commissioner of the Customs of the Port of Faversham. He removed to Faversham where he lived in part of the abbey property belonging to Cheyney, and set out to make his mark and fortune. Elected Mayor in 1547, he tried to change tradition and the councillors removed him from office. Arden was afterwards murdered in his own house in 1550.

Alice Arden, his wife, was found to be a conspirator and, with her hired assassins, was tried at the abbey. She was burned to death at Canterbury, one of the conspirators was hanged at Smithfield and several more were hanged locally.

A play appeared about this time (1592) called 'The Lamentable and True Tragedy of Master Arden of Faversham in Kent' — this has been attributed to Shakespeare, following a visit by strolling players and companies, but the facts cannot be positively verified. Arden's house has since been restored to its former glory.

James II was captured here by Faversham fishermen when attempting to flee the country in the seventeenth century.

45

FOLKESTONE

Folkestone lays claim to be a rather superior seaside resort. The town is situated at the lower edge of the North Downs and is much changed by major roadways. On the sea front are large hotels, flats and boarding houses, often somewhat stylish in appearance. They overlook the harbour where cross-channel traffic continually may be seen. The harbour has its own station and from here small, often cobbled and twisting streets run up into central Folkestone. Fishing boats and pleasure craft complete a pleasant and fairly typical harbour setting.

The Leas sea front stretches south westwards to Sandgate and on to Hythe and the marshes.

William Harvey, discoverer of the blood circulation system in the human body, was born here. In the church lies St Eanswythe, daughter of the son of King Ethelbert.

The Harbour

FORDWICH

Fordwich, although small, is a town of considerable antiquity and, while its early years are obscure, it was probably a Roman settlement; even in 1961 the water supply was obtained from a Roman well. The town is mentioned in the Domesday Survey and was listed as a borough until 1886.

Fordwich is known as the port of Canterbury, situated some two miles from the city along the course of the River Stour. As in the case of many small ports along this coast, it was a limb of another port (Sandwich) which in turn was one of the Cinque Ports with the parishioners contributing towards the cost of the ships — the forerunners of the Royal Navy.

The buildings of the town that are of interest are the Town Hall close by the church and Crane House with its crane projecting over the quay.

Many flint hand tools and axes have been found in the gravel here. In the Town Hall, (repaired in 1474) may be seen the ducking stool, and drums used by the Press Gang.

FRITTENDEN

Frittenden itself has little claim upon our attention but within its immediate surroundings may be found some fine timbered dwellings, old farms and hamlets. Within easy reach too are the more architecturally remarkable Wealden villages of Cranbrook, Biddenden, Staplehurst and Headcorn.

Hasted, the Kentish antiquarian, informs us that Frittenden was once part of the priory at Leeds until the latter's suppression during the reign of Henry VIII when it was transferred to the Crown.

Writing in 1798 Hasted further tells us that the parish comprised seventy houses and the soil was "a deep clay unkind for tillage — the occupiers have but little produce from their lands which consequently keeps them very poor."

The village is on the Beult, and Roman urns have been found here.

GODMERSHAM

Still journeying along the banks of the River Stour we come across Godmersham. Here is the Park, often visited by Jane Austen, with the settlement deriving its name from the Saxon Godmer. The village passed to the Austen family during the reign of Richard II. The various manors of Godmersham were divided between several wealthy persons and Thomas Brodnax who inherited some money and later built the manor at Godmersham Park. His son married into the well-known Kentish family, the Knatchbulls.

The saga continues with the Austen family living at Horsmonden, George Austen entering the church in 1700. The aforementioned Brodnax (who later changed his name to Knight) was a distant relative and gave to Austen the parish of Steventon near Basingstoke. The seventh of his eight children was Jane Austen. Her brother, Edward, who was friendly with the Knights at Godmersham, was bequeathed the Park in 1794. Jane often visited her brother and recorded its atmosphere in her literary work.

One should take time to visit the church for it has a pleasing Norman tower and a late twelfth century sculpture whose subject is uncertain but was possibly the murdered Thomas Becket.

The Park

GOUDHURST

Records show that there were settlements at Goudhurst over a thousand years ago. Part of the very word, Goudhurst, means a wooded eminence or clearing and ancient trackways have been uncovered. Goudhurst is not mentioned in the Domesday Book even though the church is a mere four years younger.

During the fourteenth century, the Flemish weavers came to the Weald, to Goudhurst, and stayed there for over three centuries; certainly Tudor Goudhurst must have been a very busy place with cloth-making and weaving featuring prominently. The church has some fine Culpeper monuments.

Goudhurst church is also much larger than village churches usually are due to this medieval growth. It stands high in the village on a dangerous bend in the road.

Another village occupation was that of iron founding, the subject of Ernest Straker's comprehensive book, *Wealden Iron*, and, with the hop harvest, came the annual invasion of London hop-pickers, now sadly diminished; their colourful character and lively activities are much missed.

GRAVESEND 1

Gravesend is the Kentish gateway to the Thames esturary. Here we
have rounded the marshy peninsula of Hoo and Grain and head
inland once more for the Pool of London. It is from here that the
pilots commence their river journey past the industrial areas of
Northfleet and Dartford and on to the relaxing vista of Greenwich.

There is little of antiquity left in Gravesend; most of the
buildings are new and a long shopping street dissects the town. The
waterfront is extremely modest with poor wooden buildings, and it
is not difficult to imagine these narrow streets of Victorian Kent
being as infamous to the maritime fraternity as the Brook was in
Chatham.

The sea is all pervasive at Gravesend and a church has been
devoted to maritime interests — barges being the predominant
craft of the moment.

Two of the windows of St George's Church near the river
commemorate Princess Pocahontas, who lies buried nearby, Indian
princess, and daughter of Powhattan.

51

GRAVESEND 2

Gravesend was scourged by fire in the 1720s when much of the old town was destroyed. Today, commuter estates and private developments skirt the town; there is a new complex of buildings, halls and shopping facilties in the centre and only the riverfront retains its character. Traffic seems to dominate on its one way routing around the central shopping area with much vacant land utilised as temporary car parks.

Only a few weather-boarded houses remain to remind one of former times and these straddle the high street with its covered and open markets. The clock tower and the riverside gardens are pleasing to the eye in a monotonous range of shops and terraced houses.

Along the foreshore to the east and west are isolated buildings surrounded only by dismal industrial complexes.

The great Victorian soldier, General Gordon spent some happy years at Gravesend, helping poor children in addition to his military duties, and is still remembered.

The Ship and Lobster

HADLOW

One cannot avoid seeing Hadlow Tower. It is a slender, tall
structure, not of any great antiquity, defending open fields and
small villages. Could the Agricultural College require defending?
No, Hadlow Tower with its tower of around 150′ adjacent to the
church was a whim or folly. It was the wish of Walter May to be
able to view the sea some twenty miles distant.

May had constructed a rambling castle at Hadlow between the
years 1838 and 1840, and one only realises its size by looking at
contemporary prints (see Ireland's *History of Kent*). The tower is
all that is left of the castle — being octagonal in shape and four
storeyed with pinnacles. It has been abandoned for many years but
only last year it was offered on the open market for £12,500.

Hadlow Tower

HAWKHURST

A market cross once stood upon the green at the Moor, according to Edward Hasted, the Kent Historian, and "in the hedge of Beaconfield, near Beacon-lane, stood a beacon and watch house, long since taken down". At one time Hawkhurst had a less peaceable reputation, for it gave its name to the Hawkhurst Gang, a band of smugglers, who became so powerful that they virtually ruled the countryside. Led by Thomas Kingsmill, a native of Goudhurst, the Gang broke open the Custom House at Poole to recover smuggled goods, and on another occasion brutally murdered two Custom House Officers. After a number of the Gang had been hanged, and a battle had been fought at Goudhurst, between the villagers led by a former soldier, the Gang was broken up.

In the church is buried Nathaniel Lardner, a famous nonconformist divine, who was born in the village, in the Hall House in 1684, Sir John F. W. Herschel, lived for thirty years here. The third member of a family to win fame in the field of astronomy, he lies in Westminster Abbey.

Also buried here is Richard Kilburne, author of a survey of Kent in the 18th century.

54   *Typical Wealden Weatherboard, Hawkhurst*

HEADCORN

Headcorn, at the centre of the northern part of the Kentish Weald, is a gem. Seldom mentioned or written about, the architectural quality of the main street, its acute bend and the church walk make this a definite point on every traveller's itinerary.

Driving through the long main street from Maidstone towards Tenterden, one passes over the ancient bridge; along the street, past the station, the modern houses give way to several groups of timber-framed buildings including the splendid Shakespeare House with its main beams, almost unique in Kent. Next door and on either side are traditional timber buildings, and around the corner is the Old Cloth Hall, now sub-divided but nevertheless in a remarkable state of preservation.

On its return frontage, a small walkway of intimate cottages overlooks the village green, massive old oaks and St Peter and St Paul's Church. Nestling at the end of this walk is the immaculate Headcorn Manor — the best example of a Wealden house, with double bay hall, to be seen in a group setting.

All around Headcorn lie a wealth of timber-framed buildings, many described in Mason's book, *Timber-framed Houses of the Weald.*

Stephen's Bridge

HERNE

It is said that here, Nicholas Ridley, bishop and martyr first caused the Te Deum to be sung in English. The chair in which he sat is to be seen. The village has associations with the smuggling days.

The old village street gently ascends by the churchyard corner to the recently restored windmill. It appears to stand watch over St Martin's Church dating from the fourteenth century. The tower is stark and fine and dominates the remainder of the church.

Herne remains a village whilst Herne Bay across the Thanet Way has become the seaside resort with a large if somewhat elderly population. A pier and stone clock feature on the front while large hotels and guest houses also abound. A long shopping street stretches almost from Whitstable in the west to Reculver caravan park in the east.

HEVER

The earliest owners were a Norman family, de Hever, one of whom in 1340 was granted permission to crenellate. Later it passed into the hands of the de Cobham's, one of whom, Sir John, about 1380 was granted a licence to further embattle the castle. Later, in the 15th century, the castle and lands were purchased by Sir Geoffrey Bullen, a former Lord Mayor of London. His daughter Anne became the wife of Henry VIII, and Queen of England. She was later to die on the block, but by tradition is said to haunt the bridge over the Eden once a year.

In later years, the property was purchased by Mr William Waldorf Astor who restored and beautified the property, and built the attractive village adjacent to the Castle, in the Tudor style.

There is a massive gatehouse, battlements, portcullis, and machicolations to ward off marauders, but even these fortifications were not enough to oppose the wrath of Henry following Anne Boleyn's downfall. The King then presented Hever to another unfortunate wife — Anne of Cleves. Subsequent owners made few alterations prior to the resoration early this century. The splendid gardens, topiary and the Italianate garden to the rear are open to the public.

HIGHAM

Gadshill Place at Higham was the home of Charles Dickens during
his last years. Dickens was born in Portsmouth but moved at an
early age to Chatham. As a child he often walked with his father to
Gadshill Place, and noting how much he admired the house, his
father told him, that if Charles worked very hard, and became rich,
he might hope to buy that house. Eventually he did buy it, when
he had become a famous writer. Here he wrote several of his
books, and here he erected the Swiss chalet given to him by his
friend Mr Fechter. This chalet (listed Grade I) now stands in the
gardens of Rochester Museum after having been moved from the
Park at Cobham.

Gadshill is also mentioned in Shakespeare's works, as the place
where Sir John Falstaff was set upon and robbed by Prince Hal,
and Poins in the guise of highway robbers.

Gadshill Place is now an independent school for girls.

HOLLINGBOURNE

The parish of Hollingbourne is very scattered and the village is divided into two constituent sections — Eyhorne Street and the village proper at the foot of the steep scarp slope of the North Downs.

At the first bend of the minor road is Eyhorne Street and its houses fairly represent each architectural period since the sixteenth century. There is a village green behind which stands Eyhorne House where the ancient Hundred Court was held. Farther up the hill, where the Pilgrims' Way re-emerges from the narrow lanes from Thurnham, lies the Tudor manor house — now divided into luxury flats but once the home of the Culpeper family.

The Culpepers have a special chapel dedicated to the family within the church where the four daughters were in fact the chief designers of the magnificent altar cloth, brought back after the Restoration.

The son of Edward Hasted, the Kentish Historian — also named Edward — was vicar here for many years.

HYTHE

Hythe was one of the original members of the five Cinque Ports. The word 'Hythe' means landing place and, in common with much of this south-eastern part of Kent, silting occurred which resulted in harbour facilities being abandoned by 1450. Hythe did, however, receive its charter in the latter quarter of the sixteenth century and continued to prosper.

Hythe Church is of interest largely on account of its crypt containing many skulls, supposedly those of Britons or Danes slain about 456 AD. In a grave in the churchyard lies Lionel Lukin, obit 1788, pioneer of the lifeboat.

Hythe is at the head of the Royal Military Canal running almost to Rye where a mini-Venetian carnival is held every two years, described so well in H G Wells' book *Kipps*.

The town is also the principal station on the Romney, Hythe and Dymchurch miniature railway running to Dungeness.

Close by Hythe is Saltwood Castle dating from Norman times, rebuilt about 1160 and added to during the fourteenth century. It is here that the murderers of Becket are supposed to have finalised their fiendish plot.

IGHTHAM

Ightham Mote, like Hever and Bodiam castles, is surrounded by
water and is possibly one of the finest moated houses in England.
The house, which is open to the public, dates from the thirteenth
century and enjoys a perfect setting in a woodland clearing.

In the fifteenth century the Mote was the property of the Sheriff of
Kent and there followed a series of short-span owners until, in the
late sixteenth century, it passed to the Selby family. The principal
structure is two storeyed and of ragstone, with a central higher
entrance tower. There is the added dimension of warmth in the
timbered overhangs and the end half-timbered gabling.

Whilst in Ightham, take time to examine St Peter's Church,
Ightham Court. In the churchyard lies Benjamin Harrison, famous
antiquarian, and in the church is a monument to Dame Dorothy
Selby who is reputed to have discovered the Gunpowder Plot.
Nearby is the ancient hill fort of Oldbury Camp excavated in 1938,
and now the property of the National Trust.

61

KINGSGATE

Kingsgate is the perfect 'folly', sited perilously upon the cliff edge between Margate and Broadstairs. It is of grand design, possibly even more eccentric than Hadlow Castle near Tonbridge.

During the eighteenth century, a series of follies was erected in the area by Lord Holland, Charles Fox's father. One of the first of these was Holland House, built overlooking the bay and having originally a six-coloured Doric portico. The house was designed in the style of an Italian villa.

The castle itself was constructed about 1865 and has square and round turreted towers. Serving as an hotel, there are frequent visitors who are attracted by the nearby golf course.

Bede House was constructed close to Kingsgate on the other side of the cliff but, over the years, parts have fallen into the sea and the remains have been transformed into part of the Captain Digby Inn. Digby was formerly a notorious drinking companion of Lord Holland.

Out to sea, the passing travellers can be assured of safe passage from the light of the North Foreland Lighthouse, constructed in the late seventeenth century.

KIT'S COTY

Lying halfway up the side of the North Downs near to Aylesford and Bluebell Hill are peculiar groupings of stones. The largest of these is the megalith burial chamber called 'Kit's Coty House'. The chamber consists of four huge stones, a heavy top or capstone resting on three uprights. In days gone by the tomb was originally covered by a long barrow up to 250 feet in length. Research has shown that the burial chamber was situated at the south-eastern edge of the mound.

About half a mile further south is the group of stones known as 'Lower Kit's Coty', also known as the Countless Stones. There being a legend that it is impossible to count the stones twice without arriving at a different total each time.

Nearby is the Coffin Stone, and on the Boxley side of the Pilgrims' Way some ³₄ of a mile stands the Upper White Horse Stone, in the woods.

Since the war, a Roman villa has been excavated at Eccles.

KNOLE

A National Trust house, it stands in a large and most attractive park populated with shy fallow deer, and is a pleasant place to visit. The house was built as a courtyard house by Thomas Bourchier, Archbishop of Canterbury 1454 to 1456, buying the manor in 1456. He bequeathed it to the See, and subsequent owners extended it. Cranmer handed it over to Henry VIII, and for a brief time it was a Royal palace. Queen Elizabeth granted it to the Earl of Leicester, and eventually it came into the hands of the Sackville family. A book might be written on the history of the house alone, let alone the wonderful contents which include superb pictures, hangings, and the bedrooms of Lady Betty Germaine, and the Venetian Ambassador's Room. One can visit the house many times, and still find something fresh to admire.

LAMBERHURST

In the days of the old Wealden ironmasters, Lamberhurst was noted
for its iron workings, and not far away is the site of the furnace
where the iron railings around St Paul's were forged, at a cost of
£11,000 to the City of London. Cannon and firebacks were also
made, but the difficulty in continually finding wood to fire the
furnaces and make charcoal ended in the industry moving to the
North of England, where ample coal was to be had.

The railings around St Paul's were later taken down, and sent to
Canada, but unfortunately the ship was wrecked, and most of the
railings lost.

The village, according to Hasted, takes its name from "Lam" a
Saxon word meaning clay, and "hurst", a wood, but although this
seems reasonable, modern historians might not agree.

It was also noted at one time for its sheep, and a writer visiting the
village about 1909 talked to an old shepherd who could recall "when
forty or fifty thousand sheep were washed in a brook near here".

LEEDS

Leeds is the largest of the south-eastern fairytale castles. Only a short distance from the main Ashford to Maidstone road, constructed upon three islands in the lake which acts as the moat. The adjacent golf course spoils rather an otherwise perfect historic setting.

No longer a private residence, Leeds is open to the public at certain times of the year. Some sections of the castle's fabric date from the medieval period, and one of the earliest books to feature larger photographs is dedicated to the history of Leeds Castle.

The castle has had many owners, including the Crown and the Culpepers whose seat was at nearby Hollingbourne. One of its most curious features is that it has been used on many occasions down the ages as a prison. Some of its more famous prisoners include Richard II and up to six hundred French and Dutch prisoners of war.

In its day the castle was visited by Froissart, and one castallan was hanged outside it for denying entry to the consort of Edward II. The great Parliamentarian soldier Fairfax lived here. In later years the castle was restored by Mr. F. Wykeham-Martin, and further restored by the late Lady Baillie.

The Castle

LEIGH

St Mary's Church was consecrated during the thirteenth century
although there is little surviving of the old building. There was some
demolition during the fifteenth century but the next century saw work
commence on a tower. This was not completed until 1862 when the
tower stood firm and the walls had largely been rebuilt.

Outside the church is the half-timbered house by the lodge of Hall
Place. This is a mansion of the mid-nineteenth century, built for
Samuel Morley. Several other timbered cottages such as Ramhurst
Manor to the east of the church are pleasing to the eye.

67

LENHAM

Lenham is clustered around the village square. The scene is predominantly agricultural. To the north lies the scarp slope of the North Downs and to the south the eastern Weald. It is fitting that, in an agricultural scene, one of Lenham's most picturesque buildings should be a lowly barn rather than a stately castle.

Court Lodge Farm once possessed several barns and, although these are still structurally sound, one at least has been dismantled. Study the intricacies of the wooden construction, the joints and the mellow colours inside.

Outside is the perpendicular tower of St Mary's Church keeping a watchful eye over its village; there is a lychgate dating from medieval times, a wealden house crudely bricked over and several old houses along the Faversham road. We are in Goodsall country and are reminded of the riddle of the Saxon Warriors told in his *First Kentish Patchwork* work.

LOOSE

The village of Loose is centred on a stream along a steep-sided valley and has been called the 'Switzerland of Kent'. There is seldom snow but wooden houses abound in plenty, several being timber-framed constructions. The manor house has been well-documented by a previous owner in his book *Romances of a Tudor House* although several of these houses are in need of immediate restoration.

Loose village is no place for the car and, to be appreciated, should be visited on a crisp winter morning when a walk along the stream is enchanting and culminates in a visit to the 'Old Wool House', a heavily-timbered National Trust property. The village remains a gem in an area of little architectural interest.

SOME KENTISH WORTHIES

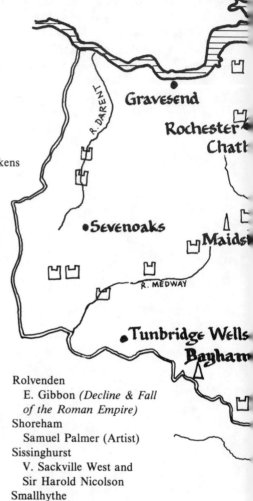

Allington
  Sir Thomas Wyatt
Aylesford
  Sir Thomas Wyatt
Bexley
  William Morris (Designer)
Boxley
  Sir Thomas Wyatt
Brenchley
  William Lambarde
Broadstairs
  Wilkie Collins and Charles Dickens
Canterbury
  Thomas Beckett,
  Christopher Marlowe
  and Charles Dickens
Chartwell
  Winston Churchill
Chatham
  Thomas Waghorn
Dartford
  R. Trevethic
Faversham
  Arden
Godmersham
  Jane Austen
Gravesend (Higham)
  Charles Dickens
Hever
  Anne Boleyn and Henry VIII
Gadshill (Higham)
  Charles Dickens
Maidstone
  William Hazlitt
Romney Marsh
  Russell Thorndyke (Dr Syn)
Penshurst
  Sir Philip Sidney
Pilgrims Way
  Chaucer
Rochester
  Charles Dickens

Rolvenden
  E. Gibbon (Decline & Fall
  of the Roman Empire)
Shoreham
  Samuel Palmer (Artist)
Sissinghurst
  V. Sackville West and
  Sir Harold Nicolson
Smallhythe
  Ellen Terry
Tenterden
  Caxton (Printer)
Tunbridge Wells
  Bean Nash
Upchurch
  Sir Francis Drake

Sheerness

Margate

Reculver

Ramsgate

tingbourne

Faversham

R. STOUR

Canterbury

Sandwich

Deal

Ashford

Dover

Folkestone

CANAL

R. ROTHER

astles   △ = Cathedrals   Abbeys & Priories

LOWER HALSTOW

These are the lost lands of Kent, neglected by progress and major development — not entirely a bad thing. The estuary of the River Medway, predominantly muddy and marshy has long been a haunt for wild life and birds. The traveller, taking the lower road to the Isle of Sheppey from the Medway towns, passes along narrow winding lanes, past hop fields and apple orchards, a sewage farm and a quay. These are the lands of the Roman potteries, of brickfields and barges.

Standing on the water's edge at Lower Halstow is the ancient church of St Margaret of Antioch. There are traces of Anglo-Saxon work here in the tiling, the nave and chancel and the splendid Norman font. Every period of church history is here displayed for the place is part-Elizabethan and the pulpit Jacobean.

There is magic in these marshes, best experienced by its chilling atmosphere in winter — visit Ham Green when the wild north-east winds are in evidence.

The Church

LYDD

Lydd is on the marsh yet has a developing international airport, a
Saxon church and a proud history. Lydd was created a town by
charter from Edward I but, like many places along this coast, the
tides and accumulating shingle have forced the River Rother to
change its course and the town has thus become less important over
the years.

The church is possibly the largest parish church in Kent, being
some 200 feet in length with its tower climbing to one hundred and
thirty feet. The tower is ragstone, of perpendicular style, and adjoins
the Early English church, unspoilt even by minor bombings of the
last war.

Lydd prospered with the local wool trade during the early Middle
Ages but there are no large cloth halls here, just in scale town houses
making up a rather sombre village which in winter looks bleak and
uninviting. This is especially so when you overlook Dungeness and
the shingle foreland which has lifeboat, lighthouse, power station and
a miniature railway. To the north at Greatstone a small holiday area
is being established.

73

MAIDSTONE 1

Maidstone is the county town as well as being the administrative and business centre of Kent. The town stands at a bridging point on the River Medway above the tidal reach of Allington Lock, and it grew from being the agricultural market place of mid-Kent. The markets are still held regularly but much of the character of Maidstone has vanished. There are modern estates and the traditional industries of brewing, corn milling and nearby paper-making.

The splendid Elizabethan Manor House, now the Museum, also contains the Regimental Museum of the Q.O.R.W.K. Regiment. In addition there are seven or eight timber-framed buildings, some with pargeting (decorative plasterwork), and the fascinating complex based around All Saints Church at the Riverside (Bishops Way). All Saints is a large church with numerous aisles, a hefty tower and splendid fitments. It was made a collegiate church about 1400 by Pope Boniface who permitted Archbishop Courteney to establish a college building consisting of an impressive Gateway and Tower, re-inforced with battlements. There is a tower abutting the river and numerous other buildings, including the Old Stables which now houses a fine collection of carriages, and was inspired by the late Sir Garrard Tyrwhitt-Drake who founded the museum.

The Old Palace, All Saints' Church and the College

MAIDSTONE 2

Within the town boundaries of Maidstone lies Mote Park. Travelling along the 'Mote Road' we descend towards the lake past the track of an outdoor model railway, past the small sailing centre where the house becomes visible. The building was erected between the years 1793 and 1801 for Lord Romney. The constructure is of fine Portland ashlar and the house is of a reasonable size and has a fine view over the lake. The principal architect was later engaged in the building of Dartmoor and Maidstone prisons!

Internally the building has large rooms, including a massive library with a fine marble chimneypiece. A pavilion, in the form of a small, round Greek temple may be found in Mote Park. The temple was erected in 1801 in honour of Lord Romney, the Lord Lieutenant of the county by the Volunteers of Kent.

Mote Park has been the home of Kent County Cricket for some years and also houses the town's modern indoor swimming pool.

William Hazlitt, essayist, critic and man of letters was born here, and much family material is in the Museum.

Mote Park

MAIDSTONE 3

Maidstone's Museum of Carriages in the centre of the county town is housed in the ancient building originally used as the Archbishop's stables. This listed building with its external staircase and crown posted roof dates from the fifteenth century and is mainly original. The restoration and alterations have only affected the brickwork over the porchway (replaced in red herringbone to contrast with the grey stone walls) and fire-proofing work. In the building can be seen landaus, royal chariots, phaetons and travelling carriages as well as four in hands, hearses and omnibuses.

H.M. the Queen has lent several vehicles from the Royal collection, making over sixty splendid vehicles housed in the museum.

MARGATE

Since the coming of the railways more than a century ago, Margate has grown to become one of the most popular coastal resorts in the south of England.

Victorian and Edwardian Margate was characterised by bathing huts and a pier; a variety of attractions have since become popular with the thousands who flock to the town every summer.

Benjamin Beale, a Quaker is credited with first introducing the bathing machine to Margate in 1753 and from this date the town developed. Initially a place visited by the nobility, its appeal is now of a much broader kind.

Be certain to visit India House built about 1770 in the older part of the town.

Margate

MEOPHAM

Meopham possesses an enormous village green and often resounds to the gentle crack of bat on ball in high summer. Overlooking the green is its windmill and some inviting cottages.

The church, dating from the twelfth century, is said to be a rebuilding of a Saxon church. This building, however, is a rebuilding of the second church as records survive to inform us of its dedication in 1325. The church lies in the middle of what is supposed to be one of the longest villages in Kent, formerly linear to the main road not unlike Staplehurst.

The smock mill, built by a Gravesend firm c.1800, is of weather boarding in contrasting black and white. It is hexagonal in shape and now well-preserved due to the efforts of local enthusiasts.

Meopham folk must be proud of their village for a wide range of pamphlets is available on such subjects as the Mill, Lost Roads, Walks and Pubs.

Meopham was the home of the Tradescant family in the seventeenth century who became renowned for their work in the botanical and natural history fields. One of the family was gardener to Charles I.

MEREWORTH

Mereworth has two major assets — the Italianate Palladian styled church and the fine castle half a mile distant, spread out along the Maidstone to Tonbridge road.

Colin Campbell completed the shell of Mereworth Castle in the year 1723, the fabric being a replica of Palladio's with rotunda. The villa in Kent was constructed for the Earl of Westmorland upon a hilltop with dual portico, originally with a moat surrounding. There is a lake, and landscaped gardens all around.

The dome-topped hundred feet square building has a long gallery with a splendid painted ceiling, several pavilions (cubed) and gatehouse lodges, separated by the present road. The Earl of Westmorland built St Lawrence's Church on its present site having previously demolished the original church which stood close to the house, in order to provide room for additional buildings.

The interior is outstanding. Truly a Palladian gem set amidst the Kentish hop fields — out of place but excusable for its perfection.

79

Yeoman's House

MILSTEAD

Standing in seclusion at the foot of the North Downs, Milstead retains much of its charm. The church perches loftily above half-timbered cottages and the Elizabethan Manor House. The finely preserved Manor House is very large with an overhang along the building. Several houses of the Wealden type lie close by St Mary's Church. The church was much affected by Victorian 'restorers' whose work included widening the north chapel and rebuilding the south chapel. Here is a long chancel and a short nave, the above mentioned chapels probably being added about 1200. The tower is an example of perpendicular type of architecture.

Interestingly in 1722 John Wyatt made land available to the parish the revenue from which was to be utilised for the education of eight poor children in the parish.

MINSTER IN THANET

The Abbey of Minster was founded c.675 by Princess Eormenburga, known to the monks as Domneva, on land given her by King Egbert of Kent, as an act of penitence for his murder of her two brothers. She became Abbess, and was succeeded by her daughter St Mildred. Following a series of Danish raids, her body was removed to Canterbury by the Abbot of St Augustine's. Later, the estates of the abbey in Thanet were given to St Augustine's, and the monks founded a grange here, called Minster Abbey, or Minster Court. They were the property of St Augustine's Abbey at Canterbury, Minster being the administrative centre of Thanet under his control and especially noted for revenue from agriculture.

Early features of its architecture are a good hall and quadrangle. The abbey and its lands were neglected in the early part of the eleventh century when they were handed over to St Augustine's and the present church was rebuilt.

81

NEWINGTON

Newington lies amidst the orchards and market gardening areas of north Kent. Here the relatively low rainfall and mild winters enable fruit and vegetables to be sent to meet the insatiable demands of the London market.

Newington is the centre of the fruit orchards and, in the centre of the village, we see the church. The construction is typically Kentish with an exceptionally fine tower and perfect proportions. It is quite a large church for a mere village with a very wide aisle and ancient chancel. The south chapel is the most fascinating — architecturally — with its crown-post construction and tiebeams. The church today, sadly, is the village. The busy main road is half a mile distant and yet these fields are tranquil and calm, providing a base for a new housing estate.

The church has a curious table tomb with four arches, said to be the shrine of St Robert of Newington.

Cherry Orchards

NEW ROMNEY

One of the Cinque Ports, it owed its origin to the decay of the ancient port of Old Romney which silted up in former times. It was bound to furnish five ships to the confederation of the Cinque Ports, together with twenty one men, and a boy. It is mentioned in Domesday Book. Its prosperity as a port ended with a great "convulsion of nature" in Edward I reign, when the river changed its course, and opened a passage to the sea at Rye. In Henry VIII's reign the town was almost two miles from the sea, and only one parish church remained. Marks of the flood water level still stain the ancient stone pillars in the church of St Nicholas.

New Romney

OFFHAM

The only surviving quintain, or jousting post, where the riders practised their tilting is to be found at Offham. There are picturesque timbered cottages clustered around the village green. King Ethelwulf granted the parish to the Church of Canterbury in the year 832 but the existing village church dates from the Norman period, evidence of which may be found in a window in the nave.

There are two houses worthy of mention, one associated with the quintain already mentioned and carrying the same name, and the two storey Manor House of purple and red brickwork.

Some of the colourful pageantry of the past, including jousting, may be experienced at the crowning of the May Queen where maypole dancing and modern attempts at tilting take place.

The Quintain

OLD ROMNEY

Romney Marsh is the land of sheep, boggy trenches and swirling mists. Bleak indeed during the winter, the area between Folkestone and Dungeness is popular with holiday makers during our short summers.

The Dungeness lifeboat and power station and a schools' holiday centre are features of the area. For those who have an inclination to wander, there are several old villages virtually untouched by the twentieth century. Farming, of course, is the prime occupation although there is additional valuable income from visiting tourists.

Old Romney lies at the heart of the marshland, where smuggling legends abound, while Martello towers and the Royal Military Canal remind one of the dangers of the invading French more than 150 years ago.

OSPRINGE

Ospringe is under threat externally and internally. From the inside it is rapidly becoming part of Faversham's westward development whilst externally traffic is a growing menace.

Despite these modern intrusions, the village retains some interesting features, including the Maison Dieu, a fifteenth century house situated at the junction of Watling Street and Water Lane, containing many relics of the past. There are old houses on both sides of Water Lane, once part of a larger complex of buildings used as a hospital, founded by Henry III in 1234. The house is open to the public and well worth an inspection, as indeed is nearby Faversham with its heritage centre, conservation area and many splendid old houses.

Returning to Ospringe, it seems usual to find the church some distance from the main street as we discovered at Newington but, after a few moments, you can see Victorian restoration work upon a building of Norman origin.

Maison Dieu

OTHAM

The village of Otham is often confused with Offham due to the local pronunciation of its name. Otham is situated some three miles to the south east of Maidstone.

There are several interesting features of this parish, notably the church which is remarkable for its parish registers dating from the 1540s. Closer scrutiny of these records reveals that burials of the day were effected in wool. The woollen industry was of paramount importance to this area as we have already seen at Cranbrook and Tenterden. In the reign of Charles II an act required that all persons should be buried in woollen material or suffer penalty of five pounds. The act even went so far as to require an affidavit to be sworn in each case. There can be little doubt that one of these 'woollen burials' was arranged for William Stevens in the year 1800. Stevens was the founder of the Society of Nobody's Friends who met "thrice annuale" and still do! He was born locally and was quite well-known as a writer and philanthropist.

There are three fine buildings in Otham. Stoneacre is a farmhouse now owned by The National Trust. Another house, even older, is Synyards (Swineyards), timber-framed and beautifully preserved and, finally, there is Gore Court Mansion dating from the reign of Henry VII.

87

PENSHURST

A visit to Penshurst is imperative. Where else is there a village offering so much to the visitor? Penshurst Place, with its lovely village setting, can rival Knole and Hever.

Penshurst Place is the home of Viscount de L'Isle VC KG and stands on the site of an older house mentioned in the Domesday Book. Sir Stephen de Penchester (associated with Allington Castle) was the first listed owner. It was in 1341 that John de Pulteney, having bought the house in 1338, obtained a licence to fortify it. His Great Hall still remains in the south. Extensions were made over the centuries by many famous people including Henry V's brother John, Duke of Bedford.

In 1521 the Crown owned the house until it passed to the Sidney family whose son, Sir Philip Sidney, became a famous Elizabethan poet and courtier. Another poet, Shelley, was seen here as grandson of a former owner. (A full description of this splendid building can be found in the Pevsner *Guide to West Kent and the Weald*).

In 1743, the Leicester line became extinct, and Penshurst descended by the female line.

PILGRIMS' WAY

Countless thousands every year make the pilgrimage to the shrine of Canterbury, and the history of the Pilgrims' Way is so well told elsewhere that it would be pointless to undertake its story here. Suffice it to say that, whilst the culmination of the Way is here in Kent, it traverses several counties.

The route is the subject of several volumes still available to the discerning browser. Julia Cartwright's book of coloured plates is probably the most comprehensive study and Hilaire Belloc's book *The Old Road* although not very accurate in a factual sense, is good reading. For the casual reader, however, the sketchbook notes by the late writer and artist Donald Maxwell is excellent value at a moderate price.

The Pilgrims' Way is not the route used by Chaucer's Pilgrims who used the Watling Street.

The Pilgrims' Way
near Wrotham

PLAXTOL

Plaxtol lies to the south of Ightham and has a thirteenth century fortified residence called 'Old Soar Manor'. This two storeyed ragstone building comprises a solar and undercroft with a chapel window shown here at the end.

There are, however, other buildings worthy of inspection, the largest of these being Fairlawne, once the residence of Sir Harry Vane, Governor of Massachusetts, beheaded 1662. His ghost is supposed to haunt the Wilderness Walk on the anniversary of his execution. For many years the house was associated with the training establishment of Royal racehorses under the late Major Peter Cazalet.

There is also Nut Tree Hall of fifteenth century, Spaite House over 600 years old and Little Damas and Old Baxted dating from Elizabethan times. The restaurant in the village, originally the forge, also dates from the fifteenth century.

The strange feature of Plaxtol is its church; an unusual construction without a name as it has never been dedicated to any saint. It was constructed principally by Archbishop Land in 1649 and several internal features are worthy of note — the seventeenth century hammerbeam rood, the carved reredos and its old pulpit.

Old Soar Manor

RAMSGATE

Thanet houses the main seaside resorts of Kent — Margate, Broadstairs and Ramsgate. All three towns possess a harbour but neither Margate nor Broadstairs can compare with the striking ramp of the wall leading down to the water's edge. Sited on the bend of the coastline, there has been a harbour at Ramsgate since Tudor times, sufficient for the Thanet fishing fleets and small repair work for the navy of the day.

The great harbour of today was started about 1750 and its importance was largely due to the notoriety of the Goodwin Sands close by and its position on the busiest trading route in the world at that time.

The special act of Parliament calling for the construction of the harbour was effected to give protection to trading vessels whilst waiting for the winds to carry them through 'The Downs'. Today the harbour is by-passed by large vessels no longer dependent upon the winds and anchorage exists only for small vessels and pleasure craft.

Today, even the harbour railway station has closed and the Dumpton miniature line is no more than a closed tunnel with the station serving as an amusement centre.

The Harbour

RECULVER

Regulbium, or Reculver, was one of the Roman forts under the command of an officer entitled The Count of the Saxon Shore, a line of defences stretching from Portchester in the south to Brancaster in the Wash area of East Anglia. All of these Roman forts are situated by the sea, of similar tough construction, and all were defended against the Saxon invasions. Reculver was adjacent to the silted up channel of the River Wantsum which at that time was an important sea route, avoiding Thanet.

The fort has fallen to the endless surge of the sea. Previous archaeologists had discovered that the fort had walls eight foot thick around a square enclosure which is protected by a ditch and earthen rampart. Today at Reculver can be seen the twin towers of King Egbert's Church constructed in AD669. Egbert was King of Kent and constructed his church within the walls of the fort. It was enlarged in the twelfth century by the addition of the second tower, and now familiar landmark to seamen throughout the world.

ROCHESTER 1

Barges were part of the Medway scene until the Cambria finally berthed at the Esplanade in Rochester and her skipper, Bob Roberts, retired. Sometimes these barges went as far west as Penzance or north to Newcastle, but they mainly plied their trade around the southern and eastern coasts. They carried all kinds of cargo and were often too well-loaded as the owners tried to make as much money as possible per voyage. Journies would often take many days, waiting for tides or changes in weather, and they fell foul of the economic climate of the 1930s when innumerable barges were berthed at Woolwich Roads. The barges, however, relied heavily on local trade, transporting cargoes of cement and bricks bound for London, and bringing return loads of rubbish, mud or chalk to be dumped around the Kent coast. In the early 1920s there were over 1500 barges operating under such well-known names as Everards, London, Rochester Trading Company and Blue Circle, skippered by such well-known names as Roberts, Horlock, Cooper, Uglow and many, many more. Most have been well-documented in biographies, reminiscences and fleet histories but there will be more books relating to barges forthcoming in 1978.

S. S. Cambria

ROCHESTER 2

Of prime importance to the development of Rochester has been its
position as a bridging point of the River Medway, allowing
travellers from the continent in days gone by to wend their way to
London and its hinterland. The Romans realised the importance of
this means of communication and constructed one of their
'motorways' naming it Watling Street. Since at any fording point
there must be elements for defence, Rochester Castle was built.
Invading troops had plundered the city by travelling up the River
Medway and the all important bridge often needed replacing.

The present castle is of Norman construction, massive, and
although now just a shell the keep at over 100 feet is the tallest
extant in England and affords splendid views from its battlements.
The castle was moated and there was a drawbridge near the present
pedestrian entrance. The walls are some seven feet thick in places
and there is a dungeon. Across the moat stands Rochester
Cathedral on the expanded site of St Andrew's Church of 604. The
present building dates from about 1200 with Gundulph's tower of
1080 remaining of the earlier construction.

ROCHESTER 3

Much has been written about Rochester and its antiquity but, at present, very little exists in print about the individual buildings of the city. Rochester has a wealth of historical buildings but little is done to encourage tourists to visit them and many of these buildings echo the general disinterest.

The castle and cathedral rightly draw much attention but others, Eastgate House in particular, need better description. Eastgate House is the city's museum but there is little of local interest here. The majority of the local objects are in store, and Dickens' Room with the quaint staircase is not accessible to the public due to new fire regulations. Moreover, the museum opens only in the afternoon.

Dickens thought more of Eastgate House than the present authorities by dedicating it as the Nun's House in *Edwin Drood*. Eastgate is a Tudor dwelling forming a group with the three timber-framed shops (originally one) opposite, and was built in 1591 by Sir Peter Buck, a paymaster in Queen Elizabeth's navy at Chatham dockyard. The river then, of course, was at the end of the garden and this would have provided the mode of transport to his work place. Much work has been done to the building and the stair case is a particularly fine feature as are the ceilings and room fittings.

95

ROCHESTER 4

Rochester High Street, which stretches from the chapel on the boundary with Chatham to the bridge over the River Medway, can be divided into upper and lower areas. The upper High Street, close by the cathedral and castle, is largely visited by tourists coming to the city who do not realise that the lower High Street too has its attractions. The western end of the High Street, is known as 'The Banks' and there are three of these with raised walkways and, originally, roads less than eight feet wide. There are houses of every architectural period here, but the middle bank contains many sixteenth and seventeenth century dwellings built from ships' timbers. These walkways were raised to protect the travellers from the rising swells of the muddy river, and it was only with the coming of the railway that the land was drained and useable. With progress and motor traffic, the 'Banks' were by-passed by the New Road running parallel but higher. On the middle bank is an interesting relic of street furniture — an old police call box.

96

ROCHESTER 5

Jasper's Gate House is one of the most photographed buildings in
the City of Rochester. The building is known by several names
including the College Gate and the Cemetery Gate. The wooden-
built upper storey which is an overhanging gable is supported by a
flint and stone archway. The main feature, the gateway, has been
lost with the demolition of the adjoining buildings and the laying
of the modern road. This gate used to be the only access to the
cathedral from the High Street at this point and, as the sketch
shows, there is a petite terrace of houses, now shops, before
reaching St Nicholas' Church. The gateway was nicknamed Jasper's
after John Jasper, in *The Mystery of Edwin Drood,* by Charles
Dickens, who lived over the archway. From here one gets a
splendid view of the massive keep of the Norman Castle and the
ditch once flanked by old houses. 97

ROCHESTER 6

The sailing barge Cambria lies by the Esplanade, and many fine
and picturesque houses are to been in the Boley Hill area,
including the Friars, Whitefriars, Langley House, and the Old Hall.
The Old Vicarage and the tiny Milton Cottage behind with its
fourteenth century wall paintings upstairs and its eleventh century
crypt below complete the group. Here we see the Castle Ditch and
the old buildings on the line of the Roman city. There is
Southgate, College Green and Priors' Gate House on the site of the
Archbishop's Palace, facing the cathedral. The gentle sweep reveals
Minor Canon Row — a splendid row of early eighteenth century
terraced residences (all listed Grade I architectural interest), and
other theological and educational buildings. In a brief space one
cannot do justice to the many historical and beautiful buildings. It
is better to wander at one's leisure, seeing them almost, by chance,
rather than through a guided tour.

ROCHESTER 7

The Archdeaconry is in fine condition and stands well with the gravel drive in front. The building was worked in red brick giving it a warmth compared to the cold grey stonework of the castle. The building comprises three main parts visible from the front. The blue-painted door stands proudly in the centre with tidy gardens to the left. There are ten windows to the central section, brick parapet with dentil banding, a blocked up window and two wings, the right hand one projecting slightly round the curve of the road.

The Headmaster's House, or Oriel House as it is more usually called, comprises three storeys and adds the dimension of height to this group of houses. Within its grounds can be seen the two-storeyed eighteenth century barn constructed of a brick base and weather-boarded first floor. There is a Dutch tiled roof with a stable door at first floor level on the front elevation. On the other side of the house is a hole through the wall giving access to The Vines, a quiet walk within a busy city.

99

ROCHESTER 8

We still have to explore St Margaret's Street and Crow Lane. In the latter lies Restoration House — a jewel in Rochester's listed crown. It is a pity that Dickens is not here to promote the preservation of his Satis House featured in *Great Expectations;* the brickwork desperately needs repair and here is a bulding which the council should purchase and open to the public. Charles II stayed here in 1660; many of its rooms are oak-panelled and there are grand fireplaces and an upstairs room where Charles II is reputed to have slept.

Rochester is blessed with many listed buildings which other cities would envy, and every effort should be made to encourage visiting tourists.

ROLVENDEN

Rolvenden, close to Tenterden, was recorded as Rovindene in the Domesday Survey. There is a predominance of weather-boarding and Kentish tile-hanging and some pleasant treescapes. There is, too, a large church with an overpowering buttress tower dating from the fifteenth century.

There are in fact two Rolvendens. Apart from the one already mentioned, there is further south Rolvenden Layne which was to provide temporary residence for the inhabitants of Rolvenden which burnt down in the late seventeenth century. The 'Layne' possesses two Tudor houses — Wesley House, where John Wesley preached in 1758, and Frensham Manor.

Hole Park, once the home of the Gibbon family (of *Decline and Fall* fame) is near the village, as is Halden Place, once the home of Lady Jane Grey.

There is a beautiful example of a post-mill at Rolvenden, the work of the late owner of Hole Park.

101

RYARSH

Ryarsh, a few miles from the Mallings, has a nice church with a typical Kentish tower, a seventeenth century pulpit and a Norman piscina. There is also close by the churchyard gate part of an enormous elm tree. It is not the fabric of the building, however, which makes this an important church but the fact that it is the burial place of a Victorian vicar who ministered the parish for thirty-eight years, one Lambert Blackerell Larking. Larking founded the Kent Archaeological Society, was its first secretary and wrote over two hundred pages for the first volume of the society's transactions, *Archaeologic Cantiana*. He also made a translation of the Domesday Book which was published after his death, and was an authority òn the Saxon language and ancient manuscripts.

Saltwood Castle

SALTWOOD

The setting of several south-eastern castles could only be described as romantic. On a grand scale there is Leeds Castle near Maidstone, Bodiam Castle just across the border and into Sussex and last, but by no means least, the smallest of all, Saltwood Castle.

The village comprises a tiny green, a medieval church with an earlier nave and the major building, the castle. The castle, although claimed after the Conquest by the clergy, has an interesting history. Archbishop Lanfranc of Canterbury was the first occupant of note. He was followed by other notable clergy, including Becket and Courtenay whose arms may be found in the great gatehouse. The first fortification is said to have been first built by Escus, or Oise, king of Kent, who succeeded his father Hengist in the year 448.

Here the four knights Reginald FitzUrse, Hugh de Moreville, William de Tracy, and Richard le Bret plotted the death of Thomas Becket, Archbishop of Canterbury. Another notable owner of the castle was Henry of Essex, Warden of the Cinque Ports and Constable of the castle, who was disgraced on the battlefield. The locality is planted with varied shrubs and plants, which give a suitably wild aspect. The castle is occupied, and is open to the public on certain occasions.

103

SANDGATE

Sandgate Castle is one of many constructed along the south-east ·
coast by Henry VIII, ever conscious of the need for strong
defences.

From the existing collection of excellent records and accounts,
we learn that the castle was built by a German, Stephan von
Haschenperg, between 1539-44 at a cost of over £5000. The basic
shape of the castle is triangular with concentric walls surrounding
the inner construction, in many respects not unlike the later
Martello towers seen fairly frequently along the Dungeness
foreland.

Near the sea stands a memorial to Sir John Moore who fell at
Corunna in 1809. Here he trained many thousands of men during
the days of the Napoleonic War.

Sandgate Castle

SANDWICH

Sandwich in winter is a bleak and forbidding place with the mist
shrouding the Barbican and the buildings offering little warmth.
One of the Cinque Ports, Sandwich stands on the Stour, and in
ancient days was bound to supply five ships for service when called
upon. Even in Lambarde's day the silting up of the haven was
causing much trouble, and in latter years only small craft can get
up to the town.

Amongst its gems are the sixteenth century Guildhall which has
some fine panelling, and many relics of the past. At one time one
might see a ducking stool there — perhaps one still can?

Despite its charm, Sandwich looks a little grimy to-day, perhaps
due to the modern traffic. It is only in recent years that the custom
of paying toll at the Barbican was abolished.

The Barbican

SCOTNEY

The borderlands of Kent and Sussex are indeed well-endowed with treasures. From the Surrey boundary and nearby Chartwell, one continues through Hever, Groombridge and the elite Tunbridge Wells eastwards to Lamberhurst, Bayham Abbey, Goudhurst and Cranbrook, then south towards Bodiam and Rye and the southeast coast.

Scotney Castle is near to Lamberhurst and lies midway between Tunbridge Wells and Hawkhurst. The gardens of the castle are the main attraction. Visited by many thousands every year, there are spendid trees and a shrubbery surrounding the fourteenth century ruins of a moated Round Tower and Tudor manor house. The author and poet Richard Church lived for some time in the Old Stable at Scotney. For many generations the house was the home of the Hussey family, and the house and lands are now National Trust property, through the generosity of the late Christopher Hussey. Mrs Hussey is in residence in the house, which is not open to view.

The Castle

SELLING

Selling lies within the Swale rural district which embraces several
hamlets — Sole Street, Shepherd's Hill, Hogben's Hill and
Shottenden Hill. These names suggest a rolling countryside so
often found in chalk landscapes — downs and weald. The scene is
agricultural with hop gardens, cherry orchards, apple orchards and
root crops.

Within the parish are the ancient monument remains of
Shottenden Hill attributed to either the Romans or the Danes.
Further south lies Sheldwich where the visitor can see Lees Court,
rebuilt after a fire, but originally designed by Inigo Jones.

107

SEVENOAKS

This town was originally called "Sevenoke" from seven oaks and in the 18th century was commonly called "Sennock". The cricket ground called The Vine is mentioned by Edward Hasted, the Kentish Historian in not very flattering words, as being "the place where the great games of Cricket, the provincial amusement of this county, are in general played".

The School is said to have been founded by an orphan child who subsequently became Lord Mayor of London. Sir William Rumpsted, about the end of Edward III's reign found the child abandoned in Sevenoaks, and with the assistance of other charitable people, educated him. Later in life, in gratitude, the William Sevenoke, as he was named, founded the School and the Alms House.

In the church lies William Lambarde, Kentish historian, and author of Perambulation of Kent.

Daniel Defoe visited the town, and mentioned it in his work on Duncan Campbell, a Scottish seer. Although no longer such a pleasant country town as formerly, it remains attractive in some respects.

Minster

SHEPPEY

The Isle of Sheppey retains its island identity still, and people from the mainland are regarded as strangers by the true islanders. The only means of getting to Sheppey is via the Kingsferry Bridge, constructed in 1961 to replace the wooden bridge which was in grave danger of collapsing under the strain of increasing modern traffic. Sheerness is today the principal town of the island.

The railway connecting the island to the mainland at Sittingbourne is just a single track spur passing through Queenborough. The latter had a castle built by Edward III who named the town after his wife. It was a defensive castle to protect the estuary and, although it never saw action, it has now almost completely vanished as has the track of the Sheppey Light Railway which connected Queenborough to the resorts of Warden and Leysdown. The track passed through Minster which has a Saxon nunnery founded in the seventh century. The nunnery existed until the Reformation and is now part of the church.

In Minster church is a memorial to Sir Robert de Shurland, upon whom Barham founded his character in his story *Grey Dolphin,* in the *Ingoldsby Legends.*

The north coast of the island is rapidly being eroded by the powerful action of the sea but the southern side remains virtually uninhabited and has lonely places such as Elmley and Harty where there is a fine church but, unfortunately, no congregation.

109

SHOREHAM

Shoreham is a pretty village along the River Darent in a valley
running from Dartford to Sevenoaks.

The area has been captured on canvas many times and, indeed
the artist Samuel Palmer lived at Water House, an eighteenth
century building in the village. There are several cottages worthy of
closer inspection before crossing the river and travelling along the
road to Dunstall Priory — an early Italianate villa. In the opposite
direction lies Filston Hall, a seventeenth century moated house.
Shoreham Castle lay one mile north of the village where now only
a farmhouse remains with its flint walling six feet thick. The castle
was obviously constructed for defence and lay along the same N-S
axis as do Eynsford and Lullingstone castles.

The writer Lord Dunsany lived here. The cross cut in the chalk
hillside commemorates the fallen of the 1914 war. Near a cross-
roads not far away a small stone in a field marks the site of an air
disaster of the 1930's.

SISSINGHURST

Sissinghurst was originally named 'Saxenhurst' and was purchased by the Baker family who built the castle during the reign of Henry VIII. Sir John Baker, its builder, was a member of the House of Commons, a Catholic and a persecutor of Protestant reformers.

Sissinghurst was visited by Queen Elizabeth I in its heyday in 1573. It declined in importance from that date and in the eighteenth century was used as a prison during the Seven Years' War. In the nineteenth century it served as the local poorhouse, and the downward trend was arrested only by the careful ownership of Sir Harold Nicolson and Lady Nicolson. Today the castle is on every tourist's itinerary and the gardens give pleasure to countless thousands every year. These gardens form the primary interest as much of the Tudor buildings have been destroyed (with the notable exception of the four storeyed gatehouse.)

111

SITTINGBOURNE

The Thames and Medway rivers were the natural home of the
russet-red sails of the barges plying their trade in the shallow
waters around the Kentish coast; in the early evening and at sunset
they made a glorious picture.

Although it is sad to reflect on the closing of a bygone age, it was
really hard work to manipulate these craft, and journies today
would be far too long if we had to wait for wind power.

There are occasions during the year when these craft can be seen
under sail — at the famous barge races or stationed at Greenwich
Pier. The yacht haven at St Katherine's Dock by the Tower offers
similar opportunities while our own Cambria, moored just by
Rochester Castle, is open to visitors during the summer. The
Cambria was the last of the barges to trade under sail and was
skippered by Bob Roberts during the golden days of barge-
building.

SMALLHYTHE

The village of Smallhythe straddles a tributary stream of the River
Rother and is situated at the southern end of the borough of
Tenterden. A quiet wayside hamlet is now all that remains of what
was once a flourishing port before silting ended Smallhythe's
maritime contracts.

One building presents itself as a tourist attraction, Smallhythe
Place, now a National Trust property. The Place is a half-timbered
yeoman's house dating from 1480. Once the home of the Chief
Officer of the port, it passed centuries later into the hands of the
celebrated actress, Dame Ellen Terry. Dame Ellen lived there for
thirty years at the turn of the century and the house is filled with
mementoes of her life. There are one or two other buildings of
some note, including the Priest's House, Yew Tree Cottage, the
restored sixteenth century ship repair dock and the Barn Theatre,
all National Trust properties. The village church is of Tudor origin.

113

SMARDEN

Smarden is a gem of a village and has often been declared the 'best kept village of the year' in Kent. There is ample proof of this from the narrow zigzag bend in the centre of the village to the heavily-timbered cottages lying adjacent to St Michael's Church. This dates from the mid-fourteenth century and its services must have been attended by endless streams of villagers giving thanks for the bountiful crops gathered from the surrounding farms.

The village of Smarden is technically a town for it was granted a licence as a market town by King Edward III in the year 1332; it did not, however, increase in size.

The delight of Smarden is not to be found in a row of houses as at Biddenden or Headcorn, but rather in its individual timber-framed houses, amongst these being Chessenden, Dragon House, Hartnup House, Thatched House and the early sixteenth century Wealden Cloth Hall.

STAPLEHURST

Staplehurst is a fine example of a linear village; for centuries its development has straddled the Maidstone-Hastings road, with isolated farmhouses further away.

The church has examples of Early English, Decorated and Perpendicular period work, the door being its best feature. This door has good Danish ironwork with a design of fishes, snakes and dragons to drive away evil spirits. There is a strange tale concerning the font; legend has it that it was discovered in a farmyard by an old blind lady who felt the object but never actually saw it nor solved the mystery of its disappearance.

There are many old timbered cottages along the High Street including Loddenden Manor, a half-timbered house standing at the end of the village, and Spilsill Court which dates from 1307.

It is at Staplehurst that the token system of change was fostered by J Simmonds. The token was usually stamped 'Staplehurst halfpenny 1794' on the face with the Kentish horse, date and amount of payment on the reverse side.

Charles Dickens was one of those who were involved in the railway disaster of 1865 at this place.

STOKE

Although the Isle of Grain has the two large industrial complexes of the power station and the oil refinery, it remains largely an unspoilt place. The Victorians had thought of developing the waterfront along the Thames as the Kentish 'Southend'. In any event, the railway passed to Port Victoria where a ferry service operated to Flushing in Holland; a branch line was opened to Allhallows some years later.

It is said that originally this line to Port Victoria was built to enable Queen Victoria to embark when visiting the Continent, — hence the name Port Victoria.

Although chalets and some amusements did come to Allhallows, it did not develop on a scale similar to Southend or Sheppey. There are still small beaches at Grain or High Halstow where in high summer it is not too crowded.

This was the 'plague and marsh fever lands' area of *Great Expectations* of Charles Dickens who frequented these country lanes.

There were plans at one time to dump much of greater London's rubbish at the Stoke 'ooze' or mudflats but, fortunately, this has not yet materialised. A splendid and isolated view of the estuary can be enjoyed from the Lower Hoo road to Stoke. The village church has a pleasing 'squat tower' — not too elaborate or too ornate — and a mile or so away at High Halstow can be found the heronry.

STONE-IN-OXNEY

The sketch depicts the Old Vicarage and St Mary's Church at the lonely parish of Stone-in-Oxney, deep in the Rother valley at the eastern most part of the Isle of Oxney. Here one has splendid views across Sussex, the marshes and the sea from Rye to Dungeness and to the hills around Folkestone.

The church stands above the village, like that at Aylesford. It is dedicated to St Mary and has a square fifteenth century tower replacing a former church destroyed by fire in the fifteenth century. One of the six church bells is of pre-Reformation date and originally belonged to St Augustine's Monastery at Canterbury.

Two items worthy of note are the Roman Mithraic altar dating from the third century adorned with the symbolic bull carved in relief. It was placed in the church in the mid-twenties after its sacrilegious use as a mounting block outside the local hostelry. Alongside the altar is an even older possession — the 130 million year old fossilised bones of a dinosaur from Stone Quarry.

Ebony to the north is a tiny island comprising 5000 acres with a scattered population totalling 500.

117

SUTTON VALENCE

Sutton Valence is a village built along the crest of the hill separating the Weald of Kent from the Vale of Holmesdale and, like its sister village, Linton, has a number of old and interesting houses. From the centre of the village with its boys' public school founded in 1576 by William Lambe, small lanes lead to the other 'Suttons', those of East and Chart.

The Rev. Cave-Brown, a prolific 'parish history writer' related the story of these two churches in one volume, although the church of East Sutton could almost be described as a chantry for East Sutton Park, home of the Royalist family, the Filmers. There are, predictably, several brasses and memorials to the family inside the church.

Traversing the winding lane back to the main village, splendid views can be obtained across the Weald and it is easy to see why the land is called the 'Garden of England'.

The castle remains here may have been built by the family of Valence, Earls of Pembroke. It has been surmised that at one time the sea came up the valley beneath the castle. An anchor found in the area several hundreds of years ago seems to confirm this story.

TENTERDEN

Romney Marsh and Tenterden in Roman times were shallow sea ports and their hinterland was the Weald, then covered by the great forest and called Andreasweald.) Some silting up and coastal shingle movement occurred during the Middle Ages and today Tenterden lies some four miles from the coast.

According to ancient legend Tenterden Steeple caused the Goodwin Sands. Money intended for the repair of a (supposed) seawall on the Isle of Lomea was spent on the steeple. The sea broke in, and the Goodwin Sands came into existence.

The town's rapid growth occurred at the time of Edward III when Flemish weavers were imported to teach their skills, and dyeing was established. Tenterden had everything — shipbuilding, port facilities and cloth industry, and it was later admitted to the confederation of Cinque Ports as a limb of Rye.

Industry and agriculture have always occupied a place of parallel importance to Tenterden but, with the silting of the port, the decline of weaving and denuding of the Wealden forest, Tenterden became less a work centre and rather more a town of fine houses and high-class shopping facilities. Caxton, the first printer in England may have lived here.

119

TESTON

At Teston (pronounced Teeson) we find yet another bridge spanning the upper Medway. The central arches of the bridge are medieval and, like Aylesford, there are small pedestrian refuges along its course. From Aylesford the river rises through Allington Locks to Maidstone Bridge and on to Barming. From here the river passes on to Teston and the bridge which serves West Farleigh. There is now another bridge to relieve the strain of modern traffic, but it is enjoyable to walk across the old one and see the river dropping by small rapids, to observe the anglers and talk to the crossing keeper who has fascinating tales to tell of ghostly hop pickers' trains leaving Maidstone and disappearing before reaching Paddock Wood.

At nearby Barham Court, Hannah Moore, William Wilberforce, and James Ramsay, vicar of Teston, and Admiral and Lady Middleton, combined to press for the abolition of slavery. A monument to Ramsay is to be seen in the church, and outside, an epitaph to a friend and servant of his, a former slave called Nestor.

TONBRIDGE

Tonbridge was the place where the Normans crossed the upper
Medway and built one of their earliest castles following the
conquest of Britain. There was a moat surrounding the site of the
prehistoric mound and in 1087 the castle was besieged by William
II. One of the defending rebel inmates (led by Odo, Earl of Kent)
included Richard de Tonbridge who was kept prisoner in
Normandy.

The castle passed eventually to the de Clare family and, under
their ownership, the massive gatehouse was built. A later rebellion
by Simon de Montfort against Henry III led to the capture of the
castle by Henry in 1264 and the burning of the town and buildings.

The Civil War saw the last defence of the castle; it has
subsequently deteriorated until now only the de Clare gatehouse
here illustrated remains.

Tonbridge is noteworthy for the great public school founded
there in 1553 by Andrew Judd. There also exist some excellent
period houses including the Portreve's House and the Chequers of
fourteenth century origin. In addition there are several fine examples
of old coaching inns, Rose and Crown, Bull, and the one beloved
of Jeffrey Farnol, the Chequers, which appears in several of his
Regency stories written in the 1930s.

121

TONGE

The parish of Tonge is bounded by two main features — the River Swale in the north and the M2 motorway in the south. Tonge is in the eastern quarter of the Kentish hop gardens and orchards and the area is one of great antiquity, having a mill recorded in the Domesday Survey (probably on the site of the existing Tonge Mill).

There is a grassy mound with a moat in the parish, all that remains of the castle which was once a stronghold of Hengist, the warrior and leader of Kent. It is here that much ancient pottery has been unearthed.

Opposite the mill and nearby castle is the weather-boarded millhouse dating from the mid-eighteenth century. The sturdy twelfth century church has a beautiful fifteenth century screen and some fine stained glass windows. The building suffered from Victorian restoration in the late nineteenth century.

TROTTISCLIFFE

Why Trottiscliffe is pronounced Trosley remains an unsolved
mystery. However, there is a warmth felt on entering the village
which, like Burnham and Detling, lies under the steep scarp of the
North Downs.

The Coldrum Stones consist of a rectangular mound with a
revetment of stones and a rectangular burial chamber. Some of the
stones have fallen out of position, and the whole has suffered over
the years. It is National Trust property and is dedicated to the
memory of the Kent antiquary Benjamin Harrison, of Ightham.
Some of the Neolithic bones, found at the site can be examined.

Trottiscliffe is an alpine-like parish rising nearly seven hundred
feet to the crest of the Downs. There was once a palace here which
belonged to the Bishop of Rochester but it has now all disappeared
except for a more modern farmhouse.

The church dates from the Norman period and the ornately-
carved pulpit once occupied a place in Westminster Abbey.

The village remains a pleasant resting place along the ancient
trackway to Canterbury for all pilgrims, ancient and modern.

123

TUNBRIDGE WELLS

The first discovery of the waters is credited to Dudley, Lord North who fell into a lingering consumptive disorder at the age of 24 and retreated from the Court to Eridge House, then a hunting seat belonging to Lord Abergavenny. Tired of life in the country he decided to return to London, and on the way noted a peculiar looking spring, and tried the water, and took some of it to London, for examination by the doctors of the day. Thus commenced the "Wells", so it is said, for people of quality came down to live in a rural manner in tents, and it became the fashion, to drink the waters. Later, booths and rustic houses were erected, and walks were laid out, and as the years passed more solid buildings were erected, and it became a Spa with a combination of water drinking, prescribed rules of life, early rising, and the usual background of scandal and gambling common to the period. Many famous people were to be seen at the Wells, the "cachet" being given by the visit of Queen Henrietta-Maria, wife of Charles I, at an early date. Over the years many local people became wealthy through the influx of visitors, and local crafts became fashionable, including the famous Tonbridge ware. Not least amongst the wealthy in the locality were the doubtful members of the medical profession who prescribed lavish doses of the waters for their patients. According to a local writer of the 18th century, up to 18 pints and 3 gills were prescribed to be drunk — in a morning! More sensible doctors prescribed a more moderate dose, but much of the reputed cures certainly lay in moderate living, early rising and exercising, as much as the waters.

The Pantiles

In 1676 a church was built by subscription on land given by Lady Purbeck, of Somerhill. Originally designated a chapel, it was later dedicated to King Charles the Martyr — much to the amusement of Thomas Benge Burr, author of a local guide book to the Wells. The church was later enlarged, and is notable for the beauty of the ceiling.

Part of Wells history influenced its growth. A fire in 1687 when the area was still in the wooden booth stage of life, burnt out much property, but subsequent rebuilding in brick and stone, to include an assembly room, led to more permanence and comfort for visitors and tradesmen. In 1688 Princess Anne of Denmark visited the Wells, and again in 1698, when leaving she left funds for the paving of the walk. Returning at a later visit, she was angered to find that nothing had been done, and left, never to return.

The Wells season ran on similar lines to that of Bath, and was presided over by Beau Nash, since the fashionable seasons of the two Spas did not clash. He introduced much the same formal rules of life, and although, naturally, not entirely disinterested himself, succeeded in raising the standard of manners and behaviour which hitherto had been somewhat crude.

With the passing of the years elegant buildings of good design by Decimus Burton, were erected, grounds and parks laid out, so that from being a modest country place, the Wells became a rather aristocratic town.

Even to-day, despite modern noise and shoddiness, a slight air of elegance still clings. It must be admitted, however, that many of the modern buildings do not harmonise with the background. Few visitors get beyond the famous Pantiles, and some still take the waters, eternally bubbling up in a stone basin. The Duchess of Kent, with the young Princess Victoria, took the waters at a visit, but it is not reported what they thought they tasted like!

Nearby are fine commons and walks, as well as great sandstone rocks, including the famous Toad Rock. The museum, housed in the Civic Centre is well worth a visit, and has many relics of the early days of the Wells.

A pedestrian precinct since the seventeenth century, The Pantiles in Tunbridge Wells combines impressive architecture and quality shopping in a peaceful environment. The original walkway was established about 1640, with the raised pavement being added about thirty years later, and is highlighted by the row of trees along its eastern edge. The usual entance to The Pantiles is from the north.

UPCHURCH

Upchurch, 2½ miles north-east of Rainham, is situated close by the marshlands and mudflats of the Medway estuary. It was once the centre of a Roman settlement and a wealth of coins and pottery has been excavated.

The centre of the village would benefit from a 'village green' as its church is somewhat hidden from view by the road and wall. The spire is unusual, comprising two stages like inverted ice cream cones. There is a tiny crypt in the church which at one time contained ancient human bones, perhaps from the Roman settlement. There is an excellent short guide to the church available at the stall in the entrance.

Upchurch's claim to fame must be through its associations with Sir Francis Drake whose father was appointed the vicar of Upchurch in 1560, and it was on the River Medway that young Francis was taught the basic skills of seamanship and navigation.

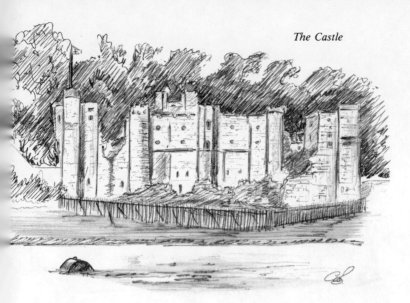

UPNOR

Upnor's naval castle was built to add an extra dimension of defence of the River Medway approaches to Rochester Castle. Elizabeth I had based her navy around Chatham Dockyard and Upnor played a major role in the defence of the yard and the many ships anchored in the sheltered waters of the Medway estuary. We have already learnt that Sir Francis Drake began his seafaring life on the waters around the Medway towns and that the timber from the Wealden forests was used for ship construction.

In 1539, when the Queen called for fortifications at Upnor, the design was entrusted to Sir Richard Lee, a famous military engineer. He employed Humphrey Locke as overseer, and the accountant for the project was Richard Watts, well-known as a local Rochester benefactor.

The castle is a water bastion, with residential block over the top, built along the riverside. There was originally a tower at each end with the gatehouse and the moat being added at a later date. The main fabric was completed between the years 1559 to 1564 with labour being the greatest cost. Much of the wood used in its construction came from Sir Thomas Wyatt's woods at Aylesford, with some stone coming from Rochester Castle.

The castle was enlarged between 1599 and 1601 and it was in 1667 that Upnor was manned and saw action when the Dutch conducted raids along the Medway.

127

The Parish Church West Malling

WEST MALLING

In the year 1090, the architect and Bishop of Rochester, Gundulf, founded a Benedictine nunnery at West Malling. There is little information generally available, however, except that it became a ruin, a house during the eighteenth century and that the Benedictine nuns have since returned. There is a gatehouse and a large and small archway with a timbered rear extension.

In 1190 the antiquarian, Gervase, reported that much of the town and Abbey of Malling were destroyed by fire and it is suggested by Newman in the survey of the buildings of West Kent and the Weald that the rebuilding was modelled on Rochester Cathedral, another of Gundulf's works.

WEST PECKHAM

There is an attractive village green at West Peckham and a tiny
parish church with a Norman tower and some traces of Saxon
stonework in its walls. The trees in the churchyard and the
overgrown surrounding wall give a welcoming appearance. The
windows are so small that they resemble arrow slits for a Norman
castle. The site of the original church was mentioned in the
Domesday Survey although, since those times, only minor
modifications have been made to the present structure. These
include the raising of the 'squire's pew', raised to first floor level in
the seventeenth century.

Close by the church is Dukes Place, a large L-shaped half-
timbered house formerly in the possession of the knights
Hospitallers to whom it was granted in 1337. The hall and the
road-end of the building were destroyed by fire in the early
sixteenth century although much of the beaming and plaster-work
are original.

Once again, local woodland has been passed over to The
National Trust for public enjoyment and there are especially fine
views from the top of Gover Hill.

129

WHITSTABLE

Whitstable, where the waters of the Swale and Medway meet again after their detour round Sheppey, owes its importance to the sea. Fishing has been one of the town's main preoccupations for over 2000 years, with particular emphasis on oyster beds. Legend has it that Julius Caesar came here looking for pearls inside the oysters and, being unseccessful, decided to use them as a food.

Whitstable possesses a harbour which was completed in 1832, just two years after the first passenger steam railway ran from Canterbury to Whitstable via the notorious Tyler Hill Tunnel. The locomotive which completed the journey was the Invicta and the engine is preserved at Canterbury. Numerous small ships use the harbour as well as the oyster boats which can be seen busily working from nearby Tankerton Castle.

Fishing Smack

WICKHAMBREUX

Wickhambreux is a pleasant village with its late fourteenth century church, old houses and, surprisingly, a working water mill.
Standing as it does by Wickham stream, the mill is a tall, weather-boarded building, painted stark white and showing well against the surrounding green courtryside.

Close by stands St Andrew's Church which is not outstanding but does have some attractive stained glass in the eastern window. It is dedicated to the Annunciation and detailed in an art nouveau style, believed to be the initial work of American artists in Europe. The approach to the church is through a pleasant avenue of lime trees surrounding the village green which is a favourite sketching place for artists.

The Church and Watermill

131

WINGHAM

Wingham, once a market town during the reign of Henry VIII, is now another large village set on a main road in East Kent and suffering from the invasion of the motor car. The village lies midway between Sandwich and Canterbury and its treelined street contains two sharp right-angled bends.

There are many fine individual timbered houses lining the main street close by the church, including Delbridge House on one side and Wingham Court on the other. Next to these are three large timber-framed buildings, at one time occupied by the canons of Wingham College. This college of secular canons was founded in 1287 and, to underline Wingham's importance, it possessed a market and a sessions' court. Much work was carried out over the centuries within the church which, being collegiate, had very ornate fittings, a fine roof and some rare if crude stonework. It is said that the pillars of the church are formed from the trunks of six chestnut trees which gratefully reflect the charm of the area in former times.

Wingham is mentioned in Shakespeare's Henry VI, part two, as being the home of one of Jack Cade's men..."there's Best's son, the tanner of Wingham".

132   *Thatched Cottage*

WOULDHAM

The tiny village of Wouldham, ranged along the waterfront between Rochester and Maidstone, has about it a rather neglected air. There are properties of all periods to be found here but most of them are unkempt and dingy. The main street with its sharp right-angled bend is cluttered with cars and empty shops.

There is the obstructed view of the River Medway and the disused barges with prefabricated cabins, long grass and unmade roads. The area is well-described in a book called *In Pilgrims' Land* originally written in 1925 by W Coles Finch, a local engineer in the Luton Waterworks Company. He tells of the (All Saints) and its tomb to Burke in whose arms Nelson died on the 'Victory'. He tells us too of the curious Starkey Castle, an old chapel transformed into a large house for Humphrey Starkey, one of Henry VII's exchequers. The house is reputed to have been built with the stone removed from the ruined archbishop's palace at Halling across the Medway.

In the church lies Major Blackburn Hart of the 95th who served in the Peninsular War under Wellington.

The Church

WYE

Wye is a small attractive market town with an equally attractive hinterland. Wye belonged to Battle Abbey after the Norman Conquest, having enjoyed Royal status during Saxon times.

The church, strangely dedicated to St Gregory and St Martin (unusual dedications in Kentish churches) was rebuilt in 1447 and endowed by Cardinal John Kempe who was to become Archbishop of Canterbury. Unfortunately, some two hundred years later the steeple collapsed and caused damage to parts of the church.

In 1432 Kempe had obtained a licence to form a college adjacent to the churchyard, traditionally planned around a quadrangle. The college, now greatly extended, has become the Agricultural College of London University, and the fact that it survived the dissolution of the monasteries was due to its being a school as well as a secular establishment.

There are many pleasant houses at Wye and, also, a mill beside the bridge crossing the River Stour en route from Canterbury to Ashford.

The first British lady novelist, Aphra Behn, was born in Wye in 1640.

The Watermill

YALDING

There is nothing more Kentish than the hop gardens and Kent used
to witness the invasion of that happy band of seasonal workers
travelling from the grime of the metropolitan industrial areas to
gather the hop harvest. Today, to a large degree, the harvesting has
become mechanised and much of the traditional good-humoured,
colourful scene has vanished.

The central areas of Kent were the most productive and here the
major breweries sited their hop farms in such rural communities as
Paddock Wood and East Farleigh. One can still see the hops being
laden at harvest time and also the 'Blossom Routes' closely
associated with the hopping industry, but only a memory of the
itinerant pickers remains written high up on the side of a house at
Barming — "Alight here for the hop gardens of Kent." Ian
Davison describes hop-picking time in his book *Where Smugglers
Walked,* the narrative of running his farm at Sissinghurst. In
another, earlier book he describes the missionary work done
amongst the hop-pickers.

Today hop oasts are converted into homes, a far cry from their
original function.

135

Oast Houses

OASTHOUSES

Oasthouses are familiar landmarks in Kent. There are a few of these buildings reputed to be over 400 years old, having been introduced from Flanders when the towns of the central Weald were the major centres of the English wool and textile industries.

The oasts are used for the skilled operation of drying the hops. In the past, teams of hop-pickers cut down the bines (now done mainly by machines) and these were transported to the machine shed in bins. Can one help but remember such evocative old terms as 'family bins', 'overseer of the sixes' (six bins in his care) and 'drift' (sixty bins)? Each drift had its 'measurer' and 'checker'; they were emptied twice a day in most fields and moved to the drying blanket ready for heating. The hops are dried for up to fourteen hours under controlled conditions to ensnare the famous flavour.